A Messian

The Daily
Torah

Daily Readings from the Torah, Haftarah and Brit Chadasha

Shemot/Exodus

Volume 2

Jeffrey K Clarke

Table of Contents

Introduction	4
Parashat Shemot	22
Parashat Bo	36
Parashat Beshalach	50
Parashat Yitro	64
Parashat Mishpatim	78
Parashat Terumah	92
Parashat Tetzaveh	106
Parashat Ki Tisa	120
Parashat Vayakhel	134
Parashat Pekudei	148

Wisdom Cries Out

My son, if you will receive my words, and store up my mitzvot within you; So as to turn your ear to wisdom, and apply your heart to understanding; Yes, if you call out for discernment, and lift up your voice for understanding; If you seek her as silver, and search for her as for hidden treasures: then you will understand the fear of the LORD, and find the knowledge of God. For the LORD gives wisdom. Out of His mouth comes knowledge and understanding. Proverbs 2:1-6

The Daily Torah: Shemot

Introduction

How To Use This Book

Blessings and shalom to you. We pray The Daily Torah readings will be enriching and spiritually uplifting to you as the Ruach HaKodesh (the Holy Spirit) leads and guides you while reading the inspired word of God on a daily basis.

Yeshua says in John 17:17 "Sanctify them in Your truth. Your word is truth."

As we seek to learn and grow in understanding, drawing closer to our Hebraic roots, let the word of God talk to you, for the word is alive and breathes. Let Him write His word in your heart.

Jeremiah says in Jer 31:31-33 Behold, the days come, says the LORD, that I will make a new covenant with the house of Yisra'el, and with the house of Yehudah: not according to the covenant that I made with their fathers in the day that I took them by the hand to bring them out of the land of Egypt; which My covenant they broke, although I was a husband to them, says the LORD. But this is the covenant that I will make with the house of Yisra'el after those days, says the LORD: I will put My law in their inward parts, and in their heart will I write it; and I will be their God, and they shall be My people..."

The Apostle Paul states: "For this cause we also thank God without ceasing, that, when you received from us the word of the message of God, you accepted it not as the word of men, but, as it is in truth, the word of God, which also works in you who believe"...(1 Thes 2:13).

History of the Torah:

God revealed the Torah through Moses. "Moses commanded us the Torah, an inheritance to the congregation of Ya'akov" (Deut. 33:4).

Unlike other prophets, Moses received his revelation clearly, not masked by symbolism. God said, "I speak to [Moses] mouth to mouth, manifestly, and not in allegory" (Numbers 12:8).

"When [I] God speak through one of you... I will speak with him in a dream. Not so My servant Moses..." (Numbers 12:6).

"God spoke to Moses face to face, as a man speaks to his friend" (Exodus 33:11).

The Torah is Eternal:

It is a foundation of our faith to believe in the eternal authority of the Torah.

"Things that are revealed belong to us and to our children forever" (Deut. 29:38).

Just as God Himself does not change, so the Torah which is His eternal testimony to Israel, cannot be changed. Moses said, "You shall not add to the word which I command you, nor shall you subtract from it; you must keep the commandments of God your Lord, which I command you" (Deut. 4:2).

The Torah scrolls that we have today are exactly the same as the Torah given to Moses by God and consist of the first five books of the Bible:

- Genesis - Bereshit
- Exodus - Shemot
- Leviticus - VaYikra
- Numbers - BaMidbar
- Deuteronomy - Devarim

History of the Torah Cycle:

During the Babylonian exile (3338-3408); 423-353 BCE), there was a decline in knowledge of the Torah. Intermarriage made headway, and many people forgot the Torah and its commandments. When Ezra and Nehemiah returned to the Holy Land, they restored the Torah to its original place. Ezra also wrote a letter perfect Torah scroll to be used as a standard and is attributed to dividing the Torah into the weekly Parasha portions.

Yeshua and the Torah:

Yeshua says "Don't think that I came to destroy the Torah or the Prophets. I didn't come to destroy, but to fulfill. For most certainly, I tell you, until heaven and earth pass away, not even one smallest letter or one tiny pen stroke shall in any way pass away from the Torah, until all things are accomplished. Whoever, therefore, shall break one of these least mitzvot, and teach others to do so, shall be called least in the Kingdom of Heaven; but whoever shall do and teach them shall be called great in the Kingdom of Heaven." (Matt 5:17-19)

Yeshua is the living Torah and during His earthly ministry, He kept it perfectly - showing us His example of not making it a burden, but a delight.

Keeping Torah is a way of life - it teaches us everything we need to know to live right, wholesome and fulfilling lives. It teaches us justice and mercy, how to love, how to handle disputes between each other, how to handle our family and work, what holy days to celebrate and how to celebrate them.

It is our instruction book, given by our Creator to guide us in all things.

Every glory and wonder, and all deep mysteries are hidden in the Torah and sealed in its treasures. There is no branch of wisdom, natural or divine, that is not contained in its depths. The Psalmist therefore prayed, "Open my eyes, so that I may behold wondrous things out of Your Torah" (Psalms 119:18).

About 'The Daily Torah':

The Daily Torah follows the weekly Parashat portions as given by Ezra the scribe, as well as the Haftarah (writings of the prophets) portions. The Brit Chadasha (renewed covenant) portions are comprised by several sources.

The Torah Cycle is based upon a lunar cycle that follows from one Simchat Torah to the next, which occurs the day after the Feast of Sukkot - held in the fall harvest season.

So beginning after Sukkot, we begin anew the Torah cycle and it continues until the next Sukkot season.

In Babylonia, the Torah was split in 54 sections and took one year to read (some portions were read together in non-leap years). The size of the sections vary, containing anywhere between 30 and more than 150 verses. The only break from the weekly cycle is when Shabbat is a Holy day with a special Torah portion.

We've tried to adhere to a 7 day cycle, but in some instances where the portions are really small, we adjust it down to 6 or 5 daily portions, and supplement special readings. Some weeks there may be double-portions.

How To Use 'The Daily Torah':

The Daily Torah has been designed in such a way as to bring us more in tune with the Hebrew calendar, but also to be re-used year after year. The Daily Torah is divided into daily reading portions for each weekly Parashat reading.

The right page contains the regular Parashat portion; the left has the Haftarah and Brit Chadasha portions.

On the headers, you'll notice the Parashat Week is displayed and the daily portion shows the verses devoted to that day.

On Holy and some non-Holy special days, there may be special readings appropriate for the day.

As you read the Daily Torah portions, pray that the Lord inspires you to see what He wants to reveal to you in His Word for that day.

All in all, we pray The Daily Torah will be a blessing to you - feel free to contact us with any comments you may have.

'The LORD bless you, and keep you.

The LORD make His face to shine on you, and be gracious to you.

The LORD lift up His face toward you, and give you shalom.' (Numbers 6:24-26)

Tzedek Shuva Ministries

Addison, TX 75001

www.tzedekshuva.org

Scriptures used: The Hebrew Names version.

Parashat Shemot - "Names"

Daily Portion: Sunday

Exodus 1:1-21

Now these are the names of the sons of Yisra'el, who came into Egypt (every man and his household came with Ya'akov): Re'uven, Shim'on, Levi, and Yehudah, Yissakhar, Zevulun, and Binyamin, Dan and Naftali, Gad and Asher. All the souls who came out of Ya'akov's body were seventy souls, and Yosef was in Egypt already. Yosef died, as did all his brothers, and all that generation.

The children of Yisra'el were fruitful, and increased abundantly, and multiplied, and grew exceedingly mighty; and the land was filled with them. Now there arose a new king over Egypt, who didn't know Yosef. He said to his people, "Behold, the people of the children of Yisra'el are more and mightier than we. Come, let us deal wisely with them, lest they multiply, and it happen that when any war breaks out, they also join themselves to our enemies, and fight against us, and escape out of the land."

Therefore they set taskmasters over them to afflict them with their burdens. They built storage cities for Par'oh: Pitom and Ra'meses. But the more they afflicted them, the more they multiplied and the more they spread out. They were grieved because of the children of Yisra'el. The Egyptians ruthlessly made the children of Yisra'el serve, and they made their lives bitter with hard service, in mortar and in brick, and in all manner of service in the field, all their service, in which they ruthlessly made them serve.

The king of Egypt spoke to the Hebrew midwives, of whom the name of the one was Shifrah, and the name of the other Pu'ah, and he said, "When you perform the duty of a midwife to the Hebrew women, and see them on the birth stool; if it is a son, then you shall kill him; but if it is a daughter, then she shall live." But the midwives feared God, and didn't do what the king of Egypt commanded them, but saved the baby boys alive.

The king of Egypt called for the midwives, and said to them, "Why have you done this thing, and have saved the boys alive?" The midwives said to Par'oh, "Because the Hebrew women aren't like the Egyptian women; for they are vigorous, and give birth before the midwife comes to them." God dealt well with the midwives, and the people multiplied, and grew very mighty. It happened, because the midwives feared God, that He gave them families.

Haftarah

Isaiah 27:6-9

Parashat Shemot — Day 1

In days to come, Ya'akov will take root. Yisra'el will blossom and bud. They will fill the surface of the world with fruit. Has He struck them as He struck those who struck them? Or are they killed like those who killed them were killed?

In measure, when you send them away, you contend with them. He has removed them with His rough blast in the day of the east wind. Therefore, by this the iniquity of Ya'akov will be forgiven, and this is all the fruit of taking away his sin: that he makes all the stones of the altar as chalk stones that are beaten in pieces, so that the Asherim and the incense altars shall rise no more.

Brit Chadasha

Luke 20:27-44

Some of the Izedukim came to Him, those who deny that there is a resurrection. They asked Him, "Rabbi, Moshe wrote to us that if a man's brother dies having a wife, and he is childless, his brother should take the wife, and raise up children for his brother.

There were therefore seven brothers. The first took a wife, and died childless. The second took her as wife, and he died childless. The third took her, and likewise the seven all left no children, and died. Afterward the woman also died. Therefore in the resurrection whose wife of them will she be? For the seven had her as a wife."

Yeshua said to them, "The children of this age marry, and are given in marriage. But those who are considered worthy to attain to that age and the resurrection from the dead, neither marry, nor are given in marriage. For they can't die any more, for they are like the angels, and are children of God, being children of the resurrection. But that the dead are raised, even Moshe showed at the bush, when he called the Lord 'The God of Avraham, the God of Yitzchak, and the God of Ya'akov.' Now He is not the God of the dead, but of the living, for all are alive to Him."

Some of the scribes answered, "Rabbi, you speak well." They didn't dare to ask Him any more questions. He said to them, "Why do they say that the Messiah is David's Son? David himself says in the book of Tehillim, 'The Lord said to my Lord, "Sit at My right hand, until I make Your enemies the footstool of Your feet."' "David therefore calls Him Lord, so how is He his son?"

The Daily Torah: Shemot / 9

Parashat Shemot - "Names"

Daily Portion: Monday

Exodus 1:22-2:20

Parashat Shemot Day 2

Par'oh charged all his people, saying, "You shall cast every son who is born into the river, and every daughter you shall save alive." A man of the house of Levi went and took a daughter of Levi as his wife. The woman conceived, and bore a son. When she saw that he was a fine child, she hid him three months.

When she could no longer hide him, she took a papyrus basket for him, and coated it with tar and with kofer. She put the child in it, and laid it in the reeds by the river's bank. His sister stood far off, to see what would be done to him. Par'oh's daughter came down to bathe at the river. Her maidens walked along by the riverside. She saw the basket among the reeds, and sent her handmaid to get it. She opened it, and saw the child, and behold, the baby cried. She had compassion on him, and said, "This is one of the Hebrews' children."

Then his sister said to Par'oh's daughter, "Should I go and call a nurse for you from the Hebrew women, that she may nurse the child for you?" Par'oh's daughter said to her, "Go." The almah went and called the child's mother. Par'oh's daughter said to her, "Take this child away, and nurse him for me, and I will give you your wages." The woman took the child, and nursed it.

The child grew, and she brought him to Par'oh's daughter, and he became her son. She named him Moshe, and said, "Because I drew him out of the water."

It happened in those days, when Moshe had grown up, that he went out to his brothers, and looked at their burdens. He saw an Egyptian striking a Hebrew, one of his brothers. He looked this way and that way, and when he saw that there was no one, he killed the Egyptian, and hid him in the sand.

He went out the second day, and behold, two men of the Hebrews were fighting with each other. He said to him who did the wrong, "Why do you strike your fellow?" He said, "Who made you a prince and a judge over us? Do you plan to kill me, as you killed the Egyptian?" Moshe was afraid, and said, "Surely this thing is known."

Now when Par'oh heard this thing, he sought to kill Moshe. But Moshe fled from the face of Par'oh, and lived in the land of Midyan, and he sat down by a well. Now the Kohen of Midyan had seven daughters.

They came and drew water, and filled the troughs to water their father's flock. The shepherds came and drove them away; but Moshe stood up and helped them, and watered their flock. When they came to Re'u'el, their father, he said,

"How is it that you have returned so early today?"

They said, "An Egyptian delivered us out of the hand of the shepherds, and moreover he drew water for us, and watered the flock."

He said to his daughters, "Where is he? Why is it that you have left the man? Call him, that he may eat bread."

> Parashat Shemot
>
> Day 2

Haftarah

Isaiah 27:10-12

For the fortified city is solitary, a habitation deserted and forsaken, like the wilderness. The calf will feed there, and there he will lie down, and consume its branches. When its boughs are withered, they will be broken off.

The women will come and set them on fire, for they are a people of no understanding.

Therefore He who made them will not have compassion on them, and He who formed them will show them no favor.

It will happen in that day, that the LORD will thresh from the flowing stream of the Perat to the brook of Egypt; and you will be gathered one by one, children of Yisra'el.

Brit Chadasha

Hebrews 11:23-27

By faith, Moshe, when he was born, was hidden for three months by his parents, because they saw that he was a beautiful child, and they were not afraid of the king's mitzvah.

By faith, Moshe, when he had grown up, refused to be called the son of Par'oh's daughter, choosing rather to share ill treatment with God's people, than to enjoy the pleasures of sin for a time; accounting the reproach of Messiah greater riches than the treasures of Egypt; for he looked to the reward.

By faith, he left Egypt, not fearing the wrath of the king; for he endured, as seeing him who is invisible.

Parashat Shemot - "Names"

Daily Portion: Tuesday

Exodus 2:21-3:12

Moshe was content to dwell with the man. He gave Moshe Tzipporah, his daughter. She bore a son, and he named him Gershom, for he said, "I have lived as a foreigner in a foreign land."

It happened in the course of those many days, that the king of Egypt died, and the children of Yisra'el sighed because of the bondage, and they cried, and their cry came up to God because of the bondage.

God heard their groaning, and God remembered His covenant with Avraham, with Yitzchak, and with Ya'akov. God saw the children of Yisra'el, and God was concerned about them.

Now Moshe was keeping the flock of Yitro, his father-in-law, the Kohen of Midyan, and he led the flock to the back of the wilderness, and came to God's mountain, to Chorev.

The angel of the LORD appeared to him in a flame of fire out of the midst of a bush. He looked, and behold, the bush burned with fire, and the bush was not consumed. Moshe said, "I will turn aside now, and see this great sight, why the bush is not burnt."

When the LORD saw that he turned aside to see, God called to him out of the midst of the bush, and said, "Moshe! Moshe!" He said, "Here I am." He said, "Don't come close. Take your sandals off of your feet, for the place you are standing on is holy ground." Moreover he said, "I am the God of your father, the God of Avraham, the God of Yitzchak, and the God of Ya`akov." Moshe hid his face; for he was afraid to look at God.

The LORD said, "I have surely seen the affliction of My people who are in Egypt, and have heard their cry because of their taskmasters, for I know their sorrows. I have come down to deliver them out of the hand of the Egyptians, and to bring them up out of that land to a good and large land, to a land flowing with milk and honey; to the place of the Kena'ani, the Chittite, the Amori, the Perizzi, the Chivvi, and the Yevusi.

Now, behold, the cry of the children of Yisra'el has come to Me. Moreover I have seen the oppression with which the Egyptians oppress them. Come now therefore, and I will send you to Par'oh, that you may bring forth My people, the children of Yisra'el, out of Egypt."

Moshe said to God, "Who am I, that I should go to Par`oh, and that I should bring forth the children of Yisra'el out of Egypt?"

He said, "Certainly I will be with you.

This will be the token to you, that I have sent you: when you have brought forth the people out of Egypt, you shall serve God on this mountain."

Parashat Shemot — Day 3

Haftarah

Isaiah 27:13-28:2

It will happen in that day that a great shofar will be blown; and those who were ready to perish in the land of Ashur, and those who were outcasts in the land of Egypt, shall come; and they will worship the LORD in the holy mountain at Yerushalayim.

Woe to the crown of pride of the drunkards of Efrayim, and to the fading flower of his glorious beauty, which is on the head of the fertile valley of those who are overcome with wine!

Behold, the Lord has a mighty and strong one. Like a storm of hail, a destroying storm, and like a storm of mighty waters overflowing, He will cast them down to the earth with His hand.

Brit Chadasha

Acts 3:12-15

When Kefa saw it, he responded to the people, "You men of Yisra'el, why do you marvel at this man? Why do you fasten your eyes on us, as though by our own power or godliness we had made him walk?

The God of Avraham, Yitzchak, and Ya'akov, the God of our fathers, has glorified His Servant Yeshua, whom you delivered up, and denied in the presence of Pilate, when he had determined to release Him.

But you denied the Holy and Righteous One, and asked for a murderer to be granted to you, and killed the Prince of life, whom God raised from the dead, to which we are witnesses."

Parashat Shemot - "Names"

Daily Portion: Wednesday

Exodus 3:13-4:5

Moshe said to God, "Behold, when I come to the children of Yisra'el, and tell them, 'The God of your fathers has sent me to you;' and they ask me, 'What is His name?' What should I tell them?"

God said to Moshe, "I AM WHO I AM," and He said, "You shall tell the children of Yisra'el this: 'I AM has sent me to you.'"

God said moreover to Moshe, "You shall tell the children of Yisra'el this, 'The LORD, the God of your fathers, the God of Avraham, the God of Yitzchak, and the God of Ya`akov, has sent me to you.'

This is My name forever, and this is My memorial to all generations. Go, and gather the elders of Yisra'el together, and tell them, 'The LORD, the God of your fathers, the God of Avraham, of Yitzchak, and of Ya`akov, has appeared to me, saying, "I have surely visited you, and seen that which is done to you in Egypt; and I have said, I will bring you up out of the affliction of Egypt to the land of the Kena'ani, the Chittite, the Amori, the Perizzi, the Chivvi, and the Yevusi, to a land flowing with milk and honey."'

They will listen to your voice, and you shall come, you and the elders of Yisra'el, to the king of Egypt, and you shall tell him, 'The LORD, the God of the Hebrews, has met with us.

Now please let us go three days' journey into the wilderness, that we may sacrifice to the LORD, our God.' I know that the king of Egypt won't give you permission to go, no, not by a mighty hand. I will put forth My hand and strike Egypt with all My wonders which I will do in the midst of it, and after that he will let you go.

I will give this people favor in the sight of the Egyptians, and it will happen that when you go, you shall not go empty-handed. But every woman shall ask of her neighbor, and of her who visits her house, jewels of silver, jewels of gold, and clothing; and you shall put them on your sons, and on your daughters. You shall despoil the Egyptians.

Moshe answered, "But, behold, they will not believe me, nor listen to my voice; for they will say, 'The LORD has not appeared to you.'" The LORD said to him, "What is that in your hand?" He said, "A rod." He said, "Throw it on the ground."

He threw it on the ground, and it became a snake; and Moshe ran away from it. The LORD said to Moshe, "Put forth your hand, and take it by the tail." He put forth his hand, and laid hold of it, and it became a rod in his hand."

That they may believe that the LORD, the God of their fathers, the God of Avraham, the God of Yitzchak, and the God of Ya`akov, has appeared to you."

Parashat Shemot Day 4

Haftarah

Isaiah 28:3-6

The crown of pride of the drunkards of Efrayim will be trodden under foot.

The fading flower of his glorious beauty, which is on the head of the fertile valley, shall be like the first-ripe fig before the summer; which someone picks and eats as soon as he sees it.

In that day, the LORD of Armies will become a crown of glory, and a diadem of beauty, to the residue of His people; and a spirit of justice to him who sits in judgment, and strength to those who turn back the battle at the gate.

Brit Chadasha

Acts 5:27-32

When they had brought them, they set them before the council. The Kohen Gadol questioned them, saying, "Didn't we strictly charge you not to teach in this name?

Behold, you have filled Yerushalayim with your teaching, and intend to bring this man's blood on us."

But Kefa and the emissaries answered, "We must obey God rather than men.

The God of our fathers raised up Yeshua, whom you killed, hanging Him on a tree.

God exalted Him with His right hand to be a Prince and a Savior, to give repentance to Yisra'el, and remission of sins.

We are His witnesses of these things; and so also is the Holy Spirit, whom God has given to those who obey Him."

Parashat Shemot - "Names"

Daily Portion: Thursday

Exodus 4:6-23

The LORD said furthermore to him, "Now put your hand inside your cloak." He put his hand inside his cloak, and when he took it out, behold, his hand was leprous, as white as snow. He said, "Put your hand inside your cloak again." He put his hand inside his cloak again, and when he took it out of his cloak, behold, it had turned again as his other flesh.

"It will happen, if they will neither believe you nor listen to the voice of the first sign, that they will believe the voice of the latter sign. It will happen, if they will not believe even these two signs, neither listen to your voice, that you shall take of the water of the river, and pour it on the dry land. The water which you take out of the river will become blood on the dry land."

Moshe said to the LORD, "Oh, Lord, I am not eloquent, neither before now, nor since you have spoken to your servant; for I am slow of speech, and of a slow tongue." The LORD said to him, "Who made man's mouth? Or who makes one mute, or deaf, or seeing, or blind? Isn't it I, the LORD? Now therefore go, and I will be with your mouth, and teach you what you shall speak." He said, "Oh, Lord, please send someone else."

The anger of the LORD was kindled against Moshe, and He said, "What about Aharon, your brother, the Levite? I know that he can speak well. Also, behold, he comes forth to meet you. When he sees you, he will be glad in his heart. You shall speak to him, and put the words in his mouth. I will be with your mouth, and with his mouth, and will teach you what you shall do. He will be your spokesman to the people; and it will happen, that he will be to you a mouth, and you will be to him as God.

You shall take this rod in your hand, with which you shall do the signs." Moshe went and returned to Yitro his father-in-law, and said to him, "Please let me go and return to my brothers who are in Egypt, and see whether they are still alive."

Yitro said to Moshe, "Go in peace." The LORD said to Moshe in Midyan, "Go, return into Egypt; for all the men who sought your life are dead." Moshe took his wife and his sons, and set them on a donkey, and he returned to the land of Egypt. Moshe took God's rod in his hand.

The LORD said to Moshe, "When you go back into Egypt, see that you do before Par`oh all the wonders which I have put in your hand, but I will harden his heart and he will not let the people go. You shall tell Par'oh, 'Thus says the LORD,

Yisra'el is My son, My firstborn, and I have said to you, "Let My son go, that he may serve Me;" and you have refused to let him go. Behold, I will kill your son, your firstborn."'

Parashat Shemot — Day 5

Haftarah

Isaiah 28:7-10 They also reel with wine, and stagger with strong drink. The Kohen and the prophet reel with strong drink. They are swallowed up by wine. They stagger with strong drink. They err in vision. They stumble in judgment. For all tables are completely full of filthy vomit and filthiness. Whom will he teach knowledge? To whom will he explain the message? Those who are weaned from the milk, and drawn from the breasts? For it is precept on precept, precept on precept; line on line, line on line; here a little, there a little.

Brit Chadasha

Acts 7:17-34 "But as the time of the promise came close which God had sworn to Avraham, the people grew and multiplied in Egypt, until there arose a different king, who didn't know Yosef. The same took advantage of our race, and mistreated our fathers, and forced them to throw out their babies, so that they wouldn't stay alive. At that time Moshe was born, and was exceedingly handsome. He was nourished three months in his father's house. When he was thrown out, Par'oh's daughter took him up, and reared him as her own son. Moshe was instructed in all the wisdom of the Egyptians. He was mighty in his words and works. But when he was forty years old, it came into his heart to visit his brothers, the children of Yisra'el. Seeing one of them suffer wrong, he defended him, and avenged him who was oppressed, striking the Egyptian. He supposed that his brothers understood that God, by his hand, was giving them deliverance; but they didn't understand. "The day following, he appeared to them as they fought, and urged them to be at peace again, saying, 'Sirs, you are brothers. Why do you wrong one another?' But he who did his neighbor wrong pushed him away, saying, 'Who made you a ruler and a Judge over us? Do you want to kill me, as you killed the Egyptian yesterday?' Moshe fled at this saying, and became a stranger in the land of Midyan, where he became the father of two sons. "When forty years were fulfilled, an angel of the Lord appeared to him in the wilderness of Mount Sinai, in a flame of fire in a bush. When Moshe saw it, he wondered at the sight. As he came close to see, a voice of the Lord came to him, 'I am the God of your fathers, the God of Avraham, the God of Yitzchak, and the God of Ya`akov.' Moshe trembled, and dared not look. The Lord said to him, 'Take your sandals off of your feet, for the place where you stand is holy ground. I have surely seen the affliction of My people that is in Egypt, and have heard their groaning. I have come down to deliver them. Now come, I will send you into Egypt.'

Parashat Shemot - "Names"

Daily Portion: Friday

Exodus 4:24-5:9

It happened on the way at a lodging place, that the LORD met him and wanted to kill him.

Then Tzipporah took a flint, and cut off the foreskin of her son, and cast it at his feet; and she said, "Surely you are a bridegroom of blood to me." So he let him alone.

Then she said, "You are a bridegroom of blood," because of the circumcision.

The LORD said to Aharon, "Go into the wilderness to meet Moshe." He went, and met him on God's mountain, and kissed him.

Moshe told Aharon all the words of the LORD with which He had sent him, and all the signs with which He had charged him.

Moshe and Aharon went and gathered together all the elders of the children of Yisra'el.

Aharon spoke all the words which the LORD had spoken to Moshe, and did the signs in the sight of the people.

The people believed, and when they heard that the LORD had visited the children of Yisra'el, and that He had seen their affliction, then they bowed their heads and worshiped.

Afterward Moshe and Aharon came, and said to Par'oh, "This is what the LORD, the God of Yisra'el, says, 'Let My people go, that they may hold a feast to Me in the wilderness.'"

Par'oh said, "Who is the LORD, that I should listen to His voice to let Yisra'el go? I don't know the LORD, and moreover I will not let Yisra'el go."

They said, "The God of the Hebrews has met with us. Please let us go three days' journey into the wilderness, and sacrifice to the LORD, our God, lest He fall on us with pestilence, or with the sword."

The king of Egypt said to them, "Why do you, Moshe and Aharon, take the people from their work? Get back to your burdens!"

Par'oh said, "Behold, the people of the land are now many, and you make them rest from their burdens."

The same day Par'oh commanded the taskmasters of the people, and their officers, saying, "You shall no longer give the people straw to make brick, as before. Let them go and gather straw for themselves.

The number of the bricks, which they made before, you require from them.

You shall not diminish anything of it, for they are idle; therefore they cry, saying, 'Let us go and sacrifice to our God.'

Let heavier work be laid on the men, that they may labor therein; and don't let them pay any attention to lying words."

> Parashat Shemot
> Day 6

Haftarah

Isaiah 28:11-13

But He will speak to this nation with stammering lips and in another language; to whom He said, "This is the resting place. Give rest to weary;" and "This is the refreshing;" yet they would not hear.

Therefore the word of the LORD will be to them precept on precept, precept on precept; line on line, line on line; here a little, there a little; that they may go, fall backward, be broken, be snared, and be taken.

Brit Chadasha

Acts 22:12-16

One Chananyah, a devout man according to the Torah, well reported of by all the Jews who lived in Damascus, came to me, and standing by me said to me, 'Brother Sha'ul, receive your sight!'

In that very hour I looked up at him. He said, 'The God of our fathers has appointed you to know His will, and to see the Righteous One, and to hear a voice from His mouth.

For you will be a witness for Him to all men of what you have seen and heard.

Now why do you wait?

Arise, be immersed, and wash away your sins, calling on the name of the Lord.'

Parashat Shemot - "Names"

Daily Portion: Shabbat

Exodus 5:10-6:1

The taskmasters of the people went out, and their officers, and they spoke to the people, saying, This is what Par'oh says: "I will not give you straw.

Go yourselves, get straw where you can find it, for nothing of your work shall be diminished."

So the people were scattered abroad throughout all the land of Egypt to gather stubble for straw.

The taskmasters were urgent saying, "Fulfill your work quota daily, as when there was straw!"

The officers of the children of Yisra'el, whom Par'oh's taskmasters had set over them, were beaten, and demanded, "Why haven't you fulfilled your quota both yesterday and today, in making brick as before?"

Then the officers of the children of Yisra'el came and cried to Par'oh, saying, "Why do you deal this way with your servants?

No straw is given to your servants, and they tell us, 'Make brick!' and behold, your servants are beaten; but the fault is in your own people."

But he said, "You are idle! You are idle! Therefore you say, 'Let us go and sacrifice to the LORD.'

Go therefore now, and work, for no straw shall be given to you, yet shall you deliver the same number of bricks!"

The officers of the children of Yisra'el saw that they were in trouble, when it was said, "You shall not diminish anything from your daily quota of bricks!"

They met Moshe and Aharon, who stood in the way, as they came forth from Par'oh: and they said to them, "May the LORD look at you, and judge, because you have made us a stench to be abhorred in the eyes of Par`oh, and in the eyes of his servants, to put a sword in their hand to kill us."

Moshe returned to the LORD, and said, "Lord, why have You brought trouble on this people? Why is it that You have sent me?

For since I came to Par'oh to speak in Your name, he has brought trouble on this people; neither have You delivered Your people at all."

The LORD said to Moshe, "Now you shall see what I will do to Par`oh, for by a strong hand he shall let them go, and by a strong hand he shall drive them out of his land."

Parashat Shemot — Day 7

Haftarah

Isaiah 29:22-23

Therefore thus says the LORD, who redeemed Avraham, concerning the house of Ya'akov: "Ya'akov shall no longer be ashamed, neither shall his face grow pale.

But when he sees his children, the work of My hands, in the midst of him, they will sanctify My name.

Yes, they will sanctify the Holy One of Ya'akov, and will stand in awe of the God of Yisra'el.

Brit Chadasha

Acts 24:14-16

But this I confess to you, that after the Way, which they call a sect, so I serve the God of our fathers, believing all things which are according to the Torah, and which are written in the prophets; having hope toward God, which these also themselves look for, that there will be a resurrection of the dead, both of the just and unjust.

Herein I also practice always having a conscience void of offense toward God and men.

Parashat: Va'era - "And I Appeared"

Daily Portion: Sunday

Parashat Va'era Day 1

Exodus 6:2-19

God spoke to Moshe, and said to him, "I am the LORD; and I appeared to Avraham, to Yitzchak, and to Ya'akov, as El Shaddai; but by My name the LORD I was not known to them.

I have also established My covenant with them, to give them the land of Kena'an, the land of their travels, in which they lived as aliens. Moreover I have heard the groaning of the children of Yisra'el, whom the Egyptians keep in bondage, and I have remembered My covenant.

Therefore tell the children of Yisra'el, 'I am the LORD, and I will bring you out from under the burdens of the Egyptians, and I will rid you out of their bondage, and I will redeem you with an outstretched arm, and with great judgments: and I will take you to Me for a people, and I will be to you a God; and you shall know that I am the LORD your God, who brings you out from under the burdens of the Egyptians.

I will bring you into the land which I swore to give to Avraham, to Yitzchak, and to Ya'akov; and I will give it to you for a heritage: I am the LORD.'" Moshe spoke so to the children of Yisra'el, but they didn't listen to Moshe for anguish of spirit, and for cruel bondage.

The LORD spoke to Moshe, saying, "Go in, speak to Par`oh king of Egypt, that he let the children of Yisra'el go out of his land." Moshe spoke before the LORD, saying, "Behold, the children of Yisra'el haven't listened to me. How then shall Par`oh listen to me, who am of uncircumcised lips?"

The LORD spoke to Moshe and to Aharon, and gave them a charge to the children of Yisra'el, and to Par'oh king of Egypt, to bring the children of Yisra'el out of the land of Egypt.

These are the heads of their fathers' houses. The sons of Re'uven the firstborn of Yisra'el: Chanokh, and Pallu, Chetzron, and Karmi; these are the families of Re'uven.

The sons of Shim'on: Yemu'el, and Yamin, and Ohad, and Yakhin, and Tzochar, and Sha'ul the son of a Kena'ani woman; these are the families of Shim'on.

These are the names of the sons of Levi according to their generations: Gershon, and Kehat, and Merari; and the years of the life of Levi were one hundred thirty-seven years.

The sons of Gershon: Livni and Shim'i, according to their families.

The sons of Kehat: 'Amram, and Yitzhar, and Chevron, and 'Uzzi'el; and the years of the life of Kehat were one hundred thirty-three years.

The sons of Merari: Machli and Mushi. These are the families of the Levites according to their generations.

Parashat Va'era — Day 1

Haftarah
Ezekiel 28:25-26

Thus says the Lord GOD: When I shall have gathered the house of Yisra'el from the peoples among whom they are scattered, and shall be sanctified in them in the sight of the nations, then shall they dwell in their own land which I gave to My servant Ya'akov.

They shall dwell securely therein; yes, they shall build houses, and plant vineyards, and shall dwell securely, when I have executed judgments on all those who do them despite round about them; and they shall know that I am the LORD their God.

Brit Chadasha
Romans 9:14-17

What shall we say then? Is there unrighteousness with God? May it never be!

For He said to Moshe, "I will have mercy on whom I have mercy, and I will have compassion on whom I have compassion."

So then it is not of him who wills, nor of him who runs, but of God who has mercy.

For the Scripture says to Par'oh, "For this very purpose I caused you to be raised up, that I might show in you My power, and that My name might be proclaimed in all the earth."

Parashat Va'era
Day 2

Parashat: Va'era - "And I Appeared"

Daily Portion: Monday

Exodus 6:20-7:7

'Amram took Yokheved his father's sister to himself as wife; and she bore him Aharon and Moshe: and the years of the life of 'Amram were a hundred and thirty-seven years.

The sons of Yitzhar: Korach, and Nefeg, and Zikhri. The sons of 'Uzzi'el: Misha'el, and Eltzafan, and Sitri. Aharon took Elisheva, the daughter of 'Amminadav, the sister of Nachshon, as his wife; and she bore him Nadav and Avihu, El'azar and Itamar.

The sons of Korach: Assir, and Elkana, and Avi'asaf; these are the families of the Korchi. El'azar Aharon's son took one of the daughters of Puti'el as his wife; and she bore him Pinechas. These are the heads of the fathers' houses of the Levites according to their families.

These are that Aharon and Moshe, to whom the LORD said, "Bring out the children of Yisra'el from the land of Egypt according to their armies." These are those who spoke to Par'oh king of Egypt, to bring out the children of Yisra'el from Egypt. These are that Moshe and Aharon.

It happened on the day when the LORD spoke to Moshe in the land of Egypt, that the LORD spoke to Moshe, saying, "I am the LORD. Speak to Par`oh king of Egypt all that I speak to you." Moshe said before the LORD, "Behold, I am of uncircumcised lips, and how shall Par`oh listen to me?"

The LORD said to Moshe, "Behold, I have made you as God to Par`oh; and Aharon your brother shall be your prophet. You shall speak all that I command you; and Aharon your brother shall speak to Par'oh, that he let the children of Yisra'el go out of his land.

I will harden Par'oh's heart, and multiply My signs and My wonders in the land of Egypt. But Par'oh will not listen to you, and I will lay My hand on Egypt, and bring forth My armies, My people the children of Yisra'el, out of the land of Egypt by great judgments.

The Egyptians shall know that I am the LORD, when I stretch forth My hand on Egypt, and bring out the children of Yisra'el from among them." Moshe and Aharon did so.

As the LORD commanded them, so they did. Moshe was eighty years old, and Aharon eighty-three years old, when they spoke to Par'oh.

Haftarah

Ezekiel 29:1-4

Parashat Va'era — Day 2

In the tenth year, in the tenth month, on the twelfth day of the month, the word of the LORD came to me, saying, "Son of man, set your face against Par`oh king of Egypt, and prophesy against him and against all Egypt.

Speak and say, 'Thus says the Lord GOD: "Behold, I am against you, Par`oh king of Egypt, the great monster that lies in the midst of his rivers, that has said, 'My river is my own, and I have made it for myself.'

I will put hooks in your jaws, and I will make the fish of your rivers stick to your scales; and I will bring you up out of the midst of your rivers, with all the fish of your rivers which stick to your scales.

Brit Chadasha

2Corinthians 6:14-7:1

Don't be unequally yoked with unbelievers, for what fellowship have righteousness and iniquity?

Or what communion has light with darkness? What agreement has Messiah with Beliya'al?

Or what portion has a believer with an unbeliever?

What agreement has a temple of God with idols?

For you are a temple of the living God. Even as God said, "I will dwell in them, and walk in them; and I will be their God, and they will be My people."

Therefore, "'Come out from among them, and be separate,' says the Lord.

'Touch no unclean thing. I will receive you. I will be to you a Father.

You will be to Me sons and daughters,' says the Lord Almighty."

Having therefore these promises, beloved, let us cleanse ourselves from all defilement of flesh and spirit, perfecting holiness in the fear of God.

Parashat: Va'era - "And I Appeared"

Daily Portion: Tuesday

Exodus 7:8-25

The LORD spoke to Moshe and to Aharon, saying, "When Par`oh speaks to you, saying, 'Perform a miracle!' then you shall tell Aharon, 'Take your rod, and cast it down before Par`oh, that it become a serpent.'"

Moshe and Aharon went in to Par'oh, and they did so, as the LORD had commanded: and Aharon cast down his rod before Par'oh and before his servants, and it became a serpent. Then Par'oh also called for the wise men and the sorcerers. They also, the magicians of Egypt, did in like manner with their enchantments. For they cast down every man his rod, and they became serpents: but Aharon's rod swallowed up their rods.

Par'oh's heart was hardened, and he didn't listen to them; as the LORD had spoken. The LORD said to Moshe, "Par'oh's heart is stubborn. He refuses to let the people go. Go to Par'oh in the morning. Behold, he goes out to the water; and you shall stand by the river's bank to meet him; and the rod which was turned to a serpent you shall take in your hand. You shall tell him, 'The LORD, the God of the Hebrews, has sent me to you, saying, "Let My people go, that they may serve Me in the wilderness:" and behold, until now you haven't listened.

Thus says the LORD, "In this you shall know that I am the LORD. Behold, I will strike with the rod that is in my hand on the waters which are in the river, and they shall be turned to blood. The fish that are in the river shall die, and the river shall become foul; and the Egyptians shall loathe to drink water from the river."'" The LORD said to Moshe, "Tell Aharon, 'Take your rod, and stretch out your hand over the waters of Egypt, over their rivers, over their streams, and over their pools, and over all their ponds of water, that they may become blood; and there shall be blood throughout all the land of Egypt, both in vessels of wood and in vessels of stone.'"

Moshe and Aharon did so, as the LORD commanded; and he lifted up the rod, and struck the waters that were in the river, in the sight of Par'oh, and in the sight of his servants; and all the waters that were in the river were turned to blood. The fish that were in the river died; and the river became foul, and the Egyptians couldn't drink water from the river; and the blood was throughout all the land of Egypt. The magicians of Egypt did in like manner with their enchantments; and Par'oh's heart was hardened, and he didn't listen to them; as the LORD had spoken. Par'oh turned and went into his house, neither did he lay even this to heart.

All the Egyptians dug round about the river for water to drink; for they couldn't drink of the water of the river. Seven days were fulfilled, after the LORD had struck the river.

Parashat Va'era Day 3

Haftarah

Ezekiel 29:5-6

I'll cast you forth into the wilderness, you and all the fish of your rivers. You'll fall on the open field. You won't be brought together, nor gathered. I have given you for food to the animals of the earth and to the birds of the sky. All the inhabitants of Egypt will know that I am the LORD, because they have been a staff of reed to the house of Yisra'el.

Brit Chadasha

Revelation 8:1-11

When he opened the seventh seal, there was silence in heaven for about half an hour. I saw the seven angels who stand before God, and seven trumpets were given to them. Another angel came and stood over the altar, having a golden censer. Much incense was given to him, that he should add it to the prayers of all the holy ones on the golden altar which was before the throne.

The smoke of the incense, with the prayers of the holy ones, went up before God out of the angel's hand. The angel took the censer, and he filled it with the fire of the altar, and threw it on the earth. There followed thunders, sounds, lightnings, and an earthquake. The seven angels who had the seven trumpets prepared themselves to sound. The first sounded, and there followed hail and fire, mixed with blood, and they were thrown to the earth. One third of the earth was burnt up, and one third of the trees were burnt up, and all green grass was burnt up.

The second angel sounded, and something like a great burning mountain was thrown into the sea. One third of the sea became blood, and one third of the living creatures which were in the sea died. One third of the ships were destroyed. The third angel sounded, and a great star fell from the sky, burning like a torch, and it fell on one third of the rivers, and on the springs of the waters. The name of the star is called "Wormwood." One third of the waters became wormwood. Many people died from the waters, because they were made bitter.

Parashat Va'era
Day 4

Parashat: Va'era - "And I Appeared"

Daily Portion: Wednesday

Exodus 8:1-17

The LORD spoke to Moshe, Go in to Par'oh, and tell him, "This is what the LORD says, 'Let My people go, that they may serve Me. If you refuse to let them go, behold, I will plague all your borders with frogs: and the river shall swarm with frogs, which shall go up and come into your house, and into your bedchamber, and on your bed, and into the house of your servants, and on your people, and into your ovens, and into your kneading troughs: and the frogs shall come up both on you, and on your people, and on all your servants.'" The LORD said to Moshe, "Tell Aharon, 'Stretch forth your hand with your rod over the rivers, over the streams, and over the pools, and cause frogs to come up on the land of Egypt.'" Aharon stretched out his hand over the waters of Egypt; and the frogs came up, and covered the land of Egypt. The magicians did in like manner with their enchantments, and brought up frogs on the land of Egypt.

Then Par'oh called for Moshe and Aharon, and said, "Entreat the LORD, that He take away the frogs from me, and from my people; and I will let the people go, that they may sacrifice to the LORD." Moshe said to Par'oh, "I give you the honor of setting the time that I should pray for you, and for your servants, and for your people, that the frogs be destroyed from you and your houses, and remain in the river only." He said, "Tomorrow." He said, "Be it according to your word, that you may know that there is none like the LORD our God. The frogs shall depart from you, and from your houses, and from your servants, and from your people. They shall remain in the river only." Moshe and Aharon went out from Par'oh, and Moshe cried to the LORD concerning the frogs which He had brought on Par'oh. The LORD did according to the word of Moshe, and the frogs died out of the houses, out of the courts, and out of the fields.

They gathered them together in heaps, and the land stank. But when Par'oh saw that there was a respite, he hardened his heart, and didn't listen to them, as the LORD had spoken. The LORD said to Moshe, "Tell Aharon, 'Stretch out your rod, and strike the dust of the earth, that it may become lice throughout all the land of Egypt.'" They did so; and Aharon stretched out his hand with his rod, and struck the dust of the earth, and there were lice on man, and on animal; all the dust of the earth became lice throughout all the land of Egypt.

Haftarah

Ezekiel 29:7-10

When they took hold of you by your hand, you broke, and tore all their shoulders; and when they leaned on you, you broke, and paralyzed all of their thighs." Therefore thus says the Lord GOD: "Behold, I will bring a sword on you, and will cut off from you man and animal. The land of Egypt shall be a desolation and a waste; and they shall know that I am the LORD. Because he has said, 'The river is mine, and I have made it;' therefore, behold, I am against you, and against your rivers, and I will make the land of Egypt an utter waste and desolation, from Migdol to Seven even to the border of Kush.

Parashat Va'era Day 4

Brit Chadasha

Revelation 16:1-15

I heard a loud voice out of the temple, saying to the seven angels, "Go and pour out the seven bowls of the wrath of God on the earth!" The first went, and poured out his bowl into the earth, and it became a harmful and evil sore on the people who had the mark of the beast, and who worshiped his image. The second angel poured out his bowl into the sea, and it became blood as of a dead man. Every living thing in the sea died. The third poured out his bowl into the rivers and springs of water, and they became blood. I heard the angel of the waters saying, "You are righteous, who are and who were, you Holy One, because you have judged these things. For they poured out the blood of the holy ones and the prophets, and you have given them blood to drink. They deserve this." I heard the altar saying, "Yes, Lord God, the Almighty, true and righteous are your judgments."

The fourth poured out his bowl on the sun, and it was given to him to scorch men with fire. People were scorched with great heat, and people blasphemed the name of God who has the power over these plagues. They didn't repent and give him glory. The fifth poured out his bowl on the throne of the beast, and his kingdom was darkened. They gnawed their tongues because of the pain, and they blasphemed the God of heaven because of their pains and their sores. They didn't repent of their works. The sixth poured out his bowl on the great river, the Perat. Its water was dried up, that the way might be made ready for the kings that come from the sunrise. I saw coming out of the mouth of the dragon, and out of the mouth of the beast, and out of the mouth of the false prophet, three unclean spirits, something like frogs; for they are spirits of demons, performing signs; which go forth to the kings of the whole inhabited earth, to gather them together for the war of that great day of God, the Almighty. "Behold, I come like a thief. Blessed is he who watches, and keeps his clothes, so that he doesn't walk naked, and they see his shame."

Parashat Va'era
Day 5

Parashat: Va'era - "And I Appeared"

Daily Portion: Thursday

Exodus 8:18-32

The magicians tried with their enchantments to bring forth lice, but they couldn't. There were lice on man, and on animal. Then the magicians said to Par'oh, "This is the finger of God:" and Par'oh's heart was hardened, and he didn't listen to them; as the LORD had spoken. The LORD said to Moshe, "Rise up early in the morning, and stand before Par'oh; behold, he comes forth to the water; and tell him, 'This is what the LORD says, "Let My people go, that they may serve Me. Else, if you will not let My people go, behold, I will send swarms of flies on you, and on your servants, and on your people, and into your houses: and the houses of the Egyptians shall be full of swarms of flies, and also the ground whereon they are. I will set apart in that day the land of Goshen, in which My people dwell, that no swarms of flies shall be there; to the end you may know that I am the LORD in the midst of the earth.

I will put a division between My people and your people: by tomorrow shall this sign be.""" The LORD did so; and there came grievous swarms of flies into the house of Par'oh, and into his servants' houses: and in all the land of Egypt the land was corrupted by reason of the swarms of flies. Par'oh called for Moshe and for Aharon, and said, "Go, sacrifice to your God in the land!" Moshe said, "It isn't appropriate to do so; for we shall sacrifice the abomination of the Egyptians to the LORD our God. Behold, shall we sacrifice the abomination of the Egyptians before their eyes, and won't they stone us? We will go three days' journey into the wilderness, and sacrifice to the LORD our God, as He shall command us." Par'oh said, "I will let you go, that you may sacrifice to the LORD your God in the wilderness, only you shall not go very far away. Pray for me."

Moshe said, "Behold, I go out from you, and I will pray to the LORD that the swarms of flies may depart from Par`oh, from his servants, and from his people, tomorrow; only don't let Par`oh deal deceitfully any more in not letting the people go to sacrifice to the LORD." Moshe went out from Par'oh, and prayed to the LORD. The LORD did according to the word of Moshe, and He removed the swarms of flies from Par'oh, from his servants, and from his people. There remained not one. Par'oh hardened his heart this time also, and he didn't let the people go.

Haftarah

Ezekiel 29:11-16

No foot of man shall pass through it, nor foot of animal shall pass through it, neither shall it be inhabited forty years. I will make the land of Egypt a desolation in the midst of the countries that are desolate; and her cities among the cities that are laid waste shall be a desolation forty years; and I will scatter the Egyptians among the nations, and will disperse them through the countries."

> Parashat Va'era Day 5

For thus says the Lord GOD: "At the end of forty years will I gather the Egyptians from the peoples where they were scattered; and I will bring back the captivity of Egypt, and will cause them to return into the land of Patros, into the land of their birth; and they shall be there a base kingdom. It shall be the base of the kingdoms; neither shall it any more lift itself up above the nations: and I will diminish them, that they shall no more rule over the nations. It shall be no more the confidence of the house of Yisra'el, bringing iniquity to memory, when they turn to look after them: and they shall know that I am the Lord GOD.""

Brit Chadasha
Revelation 9:12-21

The first woe is past. Behold, there are still two woes coming after this. The sixth angel sounded. I heard a voice from the horns of the golden altar which is before God, saying to the sixth angel who had one shofar, "Free the four angels who are bound at the great river Perat!" The four angels were freed who had been prepared for that hour and day and month and year, so that they might kill one third of mankind. The number of the armies of the horsemen was two hundred million. I heard the number of them. Thus I saw the horses in the vision, and those who sat on them, having breastplates of fiery red, hyacinth blue, and sulfur yellow; and the heads of lions. Out of their mouths proceed fire, smoke, and sulfur.

By these three plagues were one third of mankind killed: by the fire, the smoke, and the sulfur, which proceeded out of their mouths. For the power of the horses is in their mouths, and in their tails. For their tails are like serpents, and have heads, and with them they harm. The rest of mankind, who were not killed with these plagues, didn't repent of the works of their hands, that they wouldn't worship demons, and the idols of gold, and of silver, and of brass, and of stone, and of wood; which can neither see, nor hear, nor walk. They didn't repent of their murders, nor of their sorceries, nor of their sexual immorality, nor of their thefts.

Parashat: Va'era - "And I Appeared"

Daily Portion: Friday

Parashat Va'era — Day 6

Exodus 9:1-17

Then the LORD said to Moshe, "Go in to Par`oh, and tell him, 'This is what the LORD, the God of the Hebrews, says: "Let My people go, that they may serve Me. For if you refuse to let them go, and hold them still, behold, the hand of the LORD is on your livestock which are in the field, on the horses, on the donkeys, on the camels, on the herds, and on the flocks with a very grievous pestilence. The LORD will make a distinction between the livestock of Yisra'el and the livestock of Egypt; and there shall nothing die of all that belongs to the children of Yisra'el.""'

The LORD appointed a set time, saying, "Tomorrow the LORD shall do this thing in the land." The LORD did that thing on the next day; and all the livestock of Egypt died, but of the livestock of the children of Yisra'el, not one died. Par'oh sent, and, behold, there was not so much as one of the livestock of the Yisra'eli's dead. But the heart of Par'oh was stubborn, and he didn't let the people go.

The LORD said to Moshe and to Aharon, "Take to you handfuls of ashes of the furnace, and let Moshe sprinkle it toward the sky in the sight of Par`oh. It shall become small dust over all the land of Egypt, and shall be a boil breaking forth with boils on man and on animal, throughout all the land of Egypt." They took ashes of the furnace, and stood before Par'oh; and Moshe sprinkled it up toward the sky; and it became a boil breaking forth with boils on man and on animal.

The magicians couldn't stand before Moshe because of the boils; for the boils were on the magicians, and on all the Egyptians. The LORD hardened the heart of Par'oh, and he didn't listen to them, as the LORD had spoken to Moshe. The LORD said to Moshe, "Rise up early in the morning, and stand before Par`oh, and tell him, 'This is what the LORD, the God of the Hebrews, says: "Let My people go, that they may serve Me. For this time I will send all My plagues against your heart, against your officials, and against your people; that you may know that there is none like Me in all the earth.

For now I would have put forth My hand, and struck you and your people with pestilence, and you would have been cut off from the earth; but indeed for this cause I have made you stand: to show you My power, and that My name may be declared throughout all the earth; as you still exalt yourself against My people, that you won't let them go.

Haftarah
Ezekiel 29:17-18

> Parashat Va'era
> Day 6

It came to pass in the seven and twentieth year, in the first [month], in the first [day] of the month, the word of the LORD came to me, saying, Son of man, Nevukhadnetzar 1 king of Bavel caused his army to serve a great service against Tzor: every head was made bald, and every shoulder was worn; yet had he no wages, nor his army, from Tzor, for the service that he had served against it.

Brit Chadasha
Revelation 6:1-8

I saw that the Lamb opened one of the seven seals, and I heard one of the four living creatures saying, as with a voice of thunder, "Come and see!" And behold, a white horse, and he who sat on it had a bow. A crown was given to him, and he came forth conquering, and to conquer.

When He opened the second seal, I heard the second living creature saying, "Come!" Another came forth, a red horse.

To him who sat on it was given power to take peace from the earth, and that they should kill one another. There was given to him a great sword.

When He opened the third seal, I heard the third living creature saying, "Come and see!" And behold, a black horse, and he who sat on it had a balance in his hand.

I heard a voice in the midst of the four living creatures saying, "A choenix of wheat for a denarius, and three choenix of barley for a denarius! Don't damage the oil and the wine!"

When He opened the fourth seal, I heard the fourth living creature saying, "Come and see!" And behold, a pale horse, and he who sat on it, his name was Death.

She'ol followed with him. Authority over one fourth of the earth, to kill with the sword, with famine, with death, and by the wild animals of the earth was given to him.

Parashat: Va'era - "And I Appeared"

Daily Portion: Shabbat

Exodus 9:18-35

Behold, tomorrow about this time I will cause it to rain a very grievous hail, such as has not been in Egypt since the day it was founded even until now. Now therefore command that all of your livestock and all that you have in the field be brought into shelter. Every man and animal that is found in the field, and isn't brought home, the hail shall come down on them, and they shall die."'"

Those who feared the word of the LORD among the servants of Par'oh made their servants and their livestock flee into the houses. Whoever didn't regard the word of the LORD left his servants and his livestock in the field. The LORD said to Moshe, "Stretch forth your hand toward the sky, that there may be hail in all the land of Egypt, on man, and on animal, and on every herb of the field, throughout the land of Egypt." Moshe stretched forth his rod toward the heavens, and the LORD sent thunder, hail, and lightning flashed down to the earth. The LORD rained hail on the land of Egypt. So there was very severe hail, and lightning mixed with the hail, such as had not been in all the land of Egypt since it became a nation. The hail struck throughout all the land of Egypt all that was in the field, both man and animal; and the hail struck every herb of the field, and broke every tree of the field. Only in the land of Goshen, where the children of Yisra'el were, there was no hail.

Par'oh sent, and called for Moshe and Aharon, and said to them, "I have sinned this time. The LORD is righteous, and I and my people are wicked. Pray to the LORD; for there has been enough of mighty thunderings and hail. I will let you go, and you shall stay no longer." Moshe said to him, "As soon as I have gone out of the city, I will spread abroad my hands to the LORD. The thunders shall cease, neither shall there be any more hail; that you may know that the earth is the LORD's. But as for you and your servants, I know that you don't yet fear the LORD God." The flax and the barley were struck, for the barley was in the ear, and the flax was in bloom. But the wheat and the spelt were not struck, for they had not grown up. Moshe went out of the city from Par'oh, and spread abroad his hands to the LORD; and the thunders and hail ceased, and the rain was not poured on the earth. When Par'oh saw that the rain and the hail and the thunders were ceased, he sinned yet more, and hardened his heart, he and his servants.

The heart of Par'oh was hardened, and he didn't let the children of Yisra'el go, just as the LORD had spoken through Moshe.

Haftarah

Ezekiel 29:19-21

Parashat Va'era — Day 7

Therefore thus says the Lord GOD: Behold, I will give the land of Egypt to Nevukhadnetzar 1 king of Bavel; and he shall carry off her multitude, and take her spoil, and take her prey; and it shall be the wages for his army.

I have given him the land of Egypt as his recompense for which he served, because they worked for Me, says the Lord GOD. In that day will I cause a horn to bud forth to the house of Yisra'el, and I will give you the opening of the mouth in the midst of them; and they shall know that I am the LORD.

Brit Chadasha

Revelation 6:9-17

When He opened the fifth seal, I saw underneath the altar the souls of those who had been killed for the Word of God, and for the testimony of the Lamb which they had.

They cried with a loud voice, saying, "How long, Master, the holy and true, until You judge and avenge our blood on those who dwell on the earth?" A long white robe was given to each of them. They were told that they should rest yet for a while, until their fellow servants and their brothers, who would also be killed even as they were, should complete their course.

I saw when He opened the sixth seal, and there was a great earthquake. The sun became black as sackcloth made of hair, and the whole moon became as blood. The stars of the sky fell to the earth, like a fig tree dropping its unripe figs when it is shaken by a great wind. The sky was removed like a scroll when it is rolled up. Every mountain and island were moved out of their places.

The kings of the earth, the princes, the commanding officers, the rich, the strong, and every slave and free person, hid themselves in the caves and in the rocks of the mountains.

They told the mountains and the rocks, "Fall on us, and hide us from the face of Him who sits on the throne, and from the wrath of the Lamb, for the great day of His wrath has come; and who is able to stand?"

Parashat Bo Day 1

Parashat: Bo - "Enter"

Daily Portion: Sunday

Exodus 10:1-13

The LORD said to Moshe, "Go in to Par`oh, for I have hardened his heart, and the heart of his servants, that I may show these My signs in the midst of them, and that you may tell in the hearing of your son, and of your son's son, what things I have done to Egypt, and My signs which I have done among them; that you may know that I am the LORD." Moshe and Aharon went in to Par'oh, and said to him, "This is what the LORD, the God of the Hebrews, says: 'How long will you refuse to humble yourself before Me?

Let My people go, that they may serve Me. Or else, if you refuse to let My people go, behold, tomorrow I will bring locusts into your country, and they shall cover the surface of the earth, so that one won't be able to see the earth.

They shall eat the residue of that which has escaped, which remains to you from the hail, and shall eat every tree which grows for you out of the field. Your houses shall be filled, and the houses of all your servants, and the houses of all the Egyptians; as neither your fathers nor your fathers' fathers have seen, since the day that they were on the earth to this day.'"

He turned, and went out from Par'oh. Par'oh's servants said to him, "How long will this man be a snare to us? Let the men go, that they may serve the LORD, their God. Don't you yet know that Egypt is destroyed?" Moshe and Aharon were brought again to Par'oh, and he said to them, "Go, serve the LORD your God; but who are those who will go?"

Moshe said, "We will go with our young and with our old; with our sons and with our daughters, with our flocks and with our herds will we go; for we must hold a feast to the LORD."

He said to them, "The LORD be with you if I will let you go with your little ones! See, evil is clearly before your faces. Not so! Go now you who are men, and serve the LORD; for that is what you desire!" They were driven out from Par'oh's presence.

The LORD said to Moshe, "Stretch out your hand over the land of Egypt for the locusts, that they may come up on the land of Egypt, and eat every herb of the land, even all that the hail has left." Moshe stretched forth his rod over the land of Egypt, and the LORD brought an east wind on the land all that day, and all the night; and when it was morning, the east wind brought the locusts.

Haftarah
Jeremiah 46:13-14

The word that the LORD spoke to Yirmeyahu the prophet, how that Nevukhadnetzar 1 king of Bavel should come and strike the land of Egypt. Declare you in Egypt, and publish in Migdol, and publish in Mof and in Tachpanches: say you, Stand forth, and prepare you; for the sword has devoured round about you.

Parashat Bo — Day 1

Brit Chadasha
Revelation 8:12-9:11

The fourth angel sounded, and one third of the sun was struck, and one third of the moon, and one third of the stars; so that one third of them would be darkened, and the day wouldn't shine for one third of it, and the night in the same way. I saw, and I heard an eagle, flying in mid heaven, saying with a loud voice, "Woe! Woe! Woe for those who dwell on the earth, because of the other voices of the trumpets of the three angels, who are yet to sound!"

The fifth angel sounded, and I saw a star from the sky which had fallen to the earth. The key to the pit of the abyss was given to him. He opened the pit of the abyss, and smoke went up out of the pit, like the smoke from a burning furnace. The sun and the air were darkened because of the smoke from the pit. Then out of the smoke came forth locusts on the earth, and power was given to them, as the scorpions of the earth have power. They were told that they should not hurt the grass of the earth, neither any green thing, neither any tree, but only those people who don't have God's seal on their foreheads. They were given power not to kill them, but to torment them for five months. Their torment was like the torment of a scorpion, when it strikes a person.

In those days people will seek death, and will in no way find it. They will desire to die, and death will flee from them. The shapes of the locusts were like horses prepared for war. On their heads were something like golden crowns, and their faces were like people's faces. They had hair like women's hair, and their teeth were like those of lions. They had breastplates, like breastplates of iron. The sound of their wings was like the sound of chariots, or of many horses rushing to war. They have tails like those of scorpions, and stings. In their tails they have power to harm men for five months. They have over them as king the angel of the abyss. His name in Hebrew is "Avaddon," but in Greek, he has the name "Apollyon."

Parashat Bo — Day 2

Parashat: Bo - "Enter"

Daily Portion: Monday

Exodus 10:14-29

The locusts went up over all the land of Egypt, and rested in all the borders of Egypt. They were very grievous. Before them there were no such locusts as they, neither after them shall be such.

For they covered the surface of the whole earth, so that the land was darkened, and they ate every herb of the land, and all the fruit of the trees which the hail had left. There remained nothing green, either tree or herb of the field, through all the land of Egypt.

Then Par'oh called for Moshe and Aharon in haste, and he said, "I have sinned against the LORD your God, and against you. Now therefore please forgive my sin again, and pray to the LORD your God, that He may also take away from me this death."

He went out from Par'oh, and prayed to the LORD. The LORD turned an exceeding strong west wind, which took up the locusts, and drove them into the Sea of Suf. There remained not one arbeh in all the borders of Egypt.

But the LORD hardened Par'oh's heart, and he didn't let the children of Yisra'el go. The LORD said to Moshe, "Stretch out your hand toward the sky, that there may be darkness over the land of Egypt, even darkness which may be felt."

Moshe stretched forth his hand toward the sky, and there was a thick darkness in all the land of Egypt three days. They didn't see one another, neither did anyone rise from his place for three days; but all the children of Yisra'el had light in their dwellings.

Par'oh called to Moshe, and said, "Go, serve the LORD. Only let your flocks and your herds stay behind. Let your little ones also go with you." Moshe said, "You must also give into our hand sacrifices and burnt offerings, that we may sacrifice to the LORD our God.

Our livestock also shall go with us. There shall not a hoof be left behind, for of it we must take to serve the LORD our God; and we don't know with what we must serve the LORD, until we come there."

But the LORD hardened Par'oh's heart, and He wouldn't let them go. Par'oh said to him, "Get away from me! Be careful to see my face no more; for in the day you see my face you shall die!" Moshe said, "You have spoken well. I will see your face again no more."

Haftarah

Jeremiah 46:15-17

Parashat Bo — Day 2

Why are your strong ones swept away? they didn't stand, because the LORD did drive them.

He made many to stumble, yes, they fell one on another: and they said, Arise, and let us go again to our own people, and to the land of our birth, from the oppressing sword.

They cried there, Par'oh king of Egypt is but a noise; he has let the appointed time pass by.

Brit Chadasha

Revelation 16:10-11

The fifth poured out his bowl on the throne of the beast, and his kingdom was darkened.

They gnawed their tongues because of the pain, and they blasphemed the God of heaven because of their pains and their sores.

They didn't repent of their works.

Acts 13:16-17

Sha'ul stood up, and beckoning with his hand said, "Men of Yisra'el, and you who fear God, listen.

The God of this people chose our fathers, and exalted the people when they stayed as aliens in the land of Egypt, and with an uplifted arm, He led them out of it.

Parashat Bo Day 3

Parashat: Bo - "Enter"

Daily Portion: Tuesday

Exodus 11:1-12:6

The LORD said to Moshe, "Yet one plague more will I bring on Par`oh, and on Egypt; afterwards he will let you go. When he lets you go, he will surely thrust you out altogether. Speak now in the ears of the people, and let them ask every man of his neighbor, and every woman of her neighbor, jewels of silver, and jewels of gold."

The LORD gave the people favor in the sight of the Egyptians. Moreover the man Moshe was very great in the land of Egypt, in the sight of Par'oh's servants, and in the sight of the people. Moshe said, "This is what the LORD says: 'About midnight I will go out into the midst of Egypt, and all the firstborn in the land of Egypt shall die, from the firstborn of Par'oh who sits on his throne, even to the firstborn of the female servant who is behind the mill; and all the firstborn of livestock. There shall be a great cry throughout all the land of Egypt, such as there has not been, nor shall be any more. But against any of the children of Yisra'el a dog won't even bark or move its tongue, against man or animal; that you may know that the LORD makes a distinction between the Egyptians and Yisra'el.

All these your servants shall come down to me, and bow down themselves to me, saying, "Get out, with all the people who follow you;" and after that I will go out.'" He went out from Par`oh in hot anger. The LORD said to Moshe, "Par`oh won't listen to you, that My wonders may be multiplied in the land of Egypt." Moshe and Aharon did all these wonders before Par'oh, and the LORD hardened Par'oh's heart, and he didn't let the children of Yisra'el go out of his land. The LORD spoke to Moshe and Aharon in the land of Egypt, saying, "This month shall be to you the beginning of months. It shall be the first month of the year to you.

Speak to all the congregation of Yisra'el, saying, 'On the tenth day of this month, they shall take to them every man a lamb, according to their fathers' houses, a lamb for a household; and if the household be too little for a lamb, then he and his neighbor next to his house shall take one according to the number of the souls; according to what everyone can eat you shall make your count for the lamb. Your lamb shall be without blemish, a male a year old. You shall take it from the sheep, or from the goats: and you shall keep it until the fourteenth day of the same month; and the whole assembly of the congregation of Yisra'el shall kill it at evening.

Haftarah

Jeremiah 46:18-19

As I live, says the King, whose name is the LORD of Armies, surely like Tavor among the mountains, and like Karmel by the sea, so shall he come. You daughter who dwell in Egypt, furnish yourself to go into captivity; for Mof shall become a desolation, and shall be burnt up, without inhabitant.

Parashat Bo — Day 3

Brit Chadasha

John 12:1-3

Then six days before the Pesach, Yeshua came to Beit-Anyah, where El'azar was, who had been dead, whom He raised from the dead. So they made Him a supper there. Marta served, but El'azar was one of those who sat at the table with him. Miriam, therefore, took a pound of ointment of pure nard, very precious, and anointed the feet of Yeshua, and wiped His feet with her hair. The house was filled with the fragrance of the ointment.

John 12:12-15

On the next day a great multitude had come to the feast. When they heard that Yeshua was coming to Yerushalayim, they took the branches of the palm trees, and went out to meet Him, and cried out, "Hoshia`na! Blessed is He who comes in the name of the Lord, the King of Yisra'el!" Yeshua, having found a young donkey, sat on it. As it is written, "Don't be afraid, daughter of Tziyon. Behold, your King comes, sitting on a donkey's colt."

John 12:25-32

He who loves his life will lose it. He who hates his life in this world will keep it to eternal life. If anyone serves Me, let him follow Me. Where I am, there will My servant also be. If anyone serves Me, the Father will honor him. "Now My soul is troubled. What shall I say? 'Father, save Me from this time?' But for this cause I came to this time. Father, glorify Your name!" Then there came a voice out of the sky, saying, "I have both glorified it, and will glorify it again." The multitude therefore, who stood by and heard it, said that it had thundered. Others said, "An angel has spoken to Him." Yeshua answered, "This voice hasn't come for My sake, but for your sakes. Now is the judgment of this world. Now the prince of this world will be cast out. And I, if I am lifted up from the earth, will draw all people to Myself."

Parashat: Bo - "Enter"

Daily Portion: Wednesday

Exodus 12:7-20

They shall take some of the blood, and put it on the two doorposts and on the lintel, on the houses in which they shall eat it. They shall eat the flesh in that night, roasted with fire, and matzah. They shall eat it with bitter herbs. Don't eat it raw, nor boiled at all with water, but roasted with fire; with its head, its legs and its inner parts. You shall let nothing of it remain until the morning; but that which remains of it until the morning you shall burn with fire. This is how you shall eat it: with your waist girded, your shoes on your feet, and your staff in your hand; and you shall eat it in haste: it is the LORD's Pesach. For I will go through the land of Egypt in that night, and will strike all the firstborn in the land of Egypt, both man and animal. Against all the gods of Egypt I will execute judgments: I am the LORD. The blood shall be to you for a token on the houses where you are: and when I see the blood, I will pass over you, and there shall no plague be on you to destroy you, when I strike the land of Egypt. This day shall be to you for a memorial, and you shall keep it a feast to the LORD: throughout your generations you shall keep it a feast by an ordinance forever. "'Seven days shall you eat matzah; even the first day you shall put away yeast out of your houses, for whoever eats leavened bread from the first day until the seventh day, that soul shall be cut off from Yisra'el. In the first day there shall be to you a holy convocation, and in the seventh day a holy convocation; no manner of work shall be done in them, except that which every man must eat, that only may be done by you. You shall observe the feast of matzah; for in this same day have I brought your armies out of the land of Egypt: therefore shall you observe this day throughout your generations by an ordinance forever. In the first month, on the fourteenth day of the month at evening, you shall eat matzah, until the twenty first day of the month at evening. Seven days shall there be no yeast found in your houses, for whoever eats that which is leavened, that soul shall be cut off from the congregation of Yisra'el, whether he be a foreigner, or one who is born in the land. You shall eat nothing leavened. In all your habitations you shall eat matzah.'"

Haftarah

Jeremiah 46:20-21

Egypt is a very beautiful heifer; [but] destruction out of the north is come, it is come. Also her hired men in the midst of her are like calves of the stall; for they also are turned back, they are fled away together, they didn't stand: for the day of their calamity is come on them, the time of their visitation.

Parashat Bo Day 4

Brit Chadasha

Matthew 26:17-39

Now on the first day of matzah, the talmidim came to Yeshua, saying to Him, "Where do you want us to prepare for You to eat the Pesach?" He said, "Go into the city to a certain person, and tell him, 'The Rabbi says, "My time is at hand. I will keep the Pesach at your house with My talmidim."'" The talmidim did as Yeshua commanded them, and they prepared the Pesach. Now when evening had come, He was reclining at the table with the twelve talmidim. As they were eating, He said, "Most certainly I tell you that one of you will betray Me." They were exceedingly sorrowful, and each began to ask Him, "It isn't me, is it, Lord?" He answered, "He who dipped his hand with Me in the dish, the same will betray Me. The Son of Man goes, even as it is written of him, but woe to that man through whom the Son of Man is betrayed! It would be better for that man if he had not been born." Yehudah, who betrayed Him, answered, "It isn't me, is it, Rabbi?" He said to him, "You said it." As they were eating, Yeshua took bread, gave thanks for it, and broke it. He gave to the talmidim, and said, "Take, eat; this is My body." He took the cup, gave thanks, and gave to them, saying, "All of you drink it, for this is My blood of the new covenant, which is poured out for many for the remission of sins. But I tell you that I will not drink of this fruit of the vine from now on, until that day when I drink it anew with you in My Father's Kingdom." When they had sung the Hallel, they went out to the Mount of Olives. Then Yeshua said to them, "All of you will be made to stumble because of Me tonight, for it is written, 'I will strike the shepherd, and the sheep of the flock will be scattered.' But after I am raised up, I will go before you into the Galil." But Kefa answered Him, "Even if all will be made to stumble because of You, I will never be made to stumble." Yeshua said to him, "Most certainly I tell you that tonight, before the rooster crows, you will deny Me three times." Kefa said to Him, "Even if I must die with You, I will not deny You." All of the talmidim also said likewise. Then Yeshua came with them to a place called Gat-Shemanim, and said to His talmidim, "Sit here, while I go there and pray." He took with Him Kefa and the two sons of Zavdai, and began to be sorrowful and severely troubled. Then He said to them, "My soul is exceedingly sorrowful, even to death. Stay here, and watch with Me." He went forward a little, fell on his face, and prayed, saying, "My Father, if it is possible, let this cup pass away from Me; nevertheless, not what I desire, but what You desire."

The Daily Torah: Shemot / 43

Parashat: Bo - "Enter"

Daily Portion: Thursday

Exodus 12:21-36

Then Moshe called for all the elders of Yisra'el, and said to them, "Draw out, and take lambs according to your families, and kill the Pesach. You shall take a bunch of hyssop, and dip it in the blood that is in the basin, and strike the lintel and the two doorposts with the blood that is in the basin; and none of you shall go out of the door of his house until the morning. For the LORD will pass through to strike the Egyptians; and when He sees the blood on the lintel, and on the two doorposts, the LORD will pass over the door, and will not allow the destroyer to come in to your houses to strike you. You shall observe this thing for an ordinance to you and to your sons forever. It shall happen when you have come to the land which the LORD will give you, according as He has promised, that you shall keep this service. It will happen, when your children ask you, 'What do you mean by this service?' that you shall say, 'It is the sacrifice of the LORD's Pesach, who passed over the houses of the children of Yisra'el in Egypt, when He struck the Egyptians, and spared our houses.'" The people bowed their heads and worshiped. The children of Yisra'el went and did so; as the LORD had commanded Moshe and Aharon, so they did. It happened at midnight, that the LORD struck all the firstborn in the land of Egypt, from the firstborn of Par'oh who sat on his throne to the firstborn of the captive who was in the dungeon; and all the firstborn of livestock. Par'oh rose up in the night, he, and all his servants, and all the Egyptians; and there was a great cry in Egypt, for there was not a house where there was not one dead. He called for Moshe and Aharon by night, and said, "Rise up, get out from among my people, both you and the children of Yisra'el; and go, serve the LORD, as you have said! Take both your flocks and your herds, as you have said, and be gone; and bless me also!" The Egyptians were urgent with the people, to send them out of the land in haste, for they said, "We are all dead men." The people took their dough before it was leavened, their kneading troughs being bound up in their clothes on their shoulders. The children of Yisra'el did according to the word of Moshe; and they asked of the Egyptians jewels of silver, and jewels of gold, and clothing. The LORD gave the people favor in the sight of the Egyptians, so that they let them have what they asked. They despoiled the Egyptians.

Haftarah

Jeremiah 46:22-24

The sound of it shall go like the serpent; for they shall march with an army, and come against her with axes, as wood cutters. They shall cut down her forest, says the LORD, though it can't be searched; because they are more than the locusts, and are innumerable. The daughter of Egypt shall be disappointed; she shall be delivered into the hand of the people of the north.

Parashat Bo — Day 5

Brit Chadasha

Matthew 26:59-68

Now the chief Kohanim, the elders, and the whole council sought false testimony against Yeshua, that they might put Him to death; and they found none. Even though many false witnesses came forward, they found none. But at last two false witnesses came forward, and said, "This man said, 'I am able to destroy the temple of God, and to build it in three days.'" The Kohen Gadol stood up, and said to Him, "Have You no answer? What is this that these testify against You?" But Yeshua held His shalom. The Kohen Gadol answered Him, "I adjure you by the living God, that You tell us whether You are the Messiah, the Son of God." Yeshua said to him, "You have said it. Nevertheless, I tell you, after this you will see the Son of Man sitting at the right hand of Power, and coming on the clouds of the sky." Then the Kohen Gadol tore his clothing, saying, "He has spoken blasphemy! Why do we need any more witnesses? Behold, now you have heard His blasphemy. What do you think?" They answered, "He is worthy of death!" Then they spit in His face and beat Him with their fists, and some slapped Him, saying, "Prophesy to us, You Messiah! Who hit You?"

Matthew 27:1-10

Now when morning had come, all the chief Kohanim and the elders of the people took counsel against Yeshua to put Him to death: and they bound Him, and led Him away, and delivered Him up to Pontius Pilate, the governor. Then Yehudah, who betrayed Him, when he saw that Yeshua was condemned, felt remorse, and brought back the thirty pieces of silver to the chief Kohanim and elders, saying, "I have sinned in that I betrayed innocent blood." But they said, "What is that to us? You see to it." He threw down the pieces of silver in the sanctuary, and departed. He went away and hanged himself. The chief Kohanim took the pieces of silver, and said, "It's not lawful to put them into the treasury, since it is the price of blood." They took counsel, and bought the potter's field with them, to bury strangers in. Therefore that field was called "The Field of Blood" to this day. Then that which was spoken through Yirmeyahu the prophet was fulfilled, saying, "They took the thirty pieces of silver, the price of Him upon whom a price had been set, whom some of the children of Yisra'el priced, and they gave them for the potter's field, as the Lord commanded me."

Parashat: Bo - "Enter"

Daily Portion: Friday

Exodus 12:37-13:2

The children of Yisra'el traveled from Ra'meses to Sukkot, about six hundred thousand on foot who were men, besides children. A mixed multitude went up also with them, with flocks, herds, and even very much livestock. They baked unleavened cakes of the dough which they brought forth out of Egypt; for it wasn't leavened, because they were thrust out of Egypt, and couldn't wait, neither had they prepared for themselves any food. Now the time that the children of Yisra'el lived in Egypt was four hundred thirty years. It happened at the end of four hundred thirty years, even the same day it happened, that all the armies of the LORD went out from the land of Egypt. It is a night to be much observed to the LORD for bringing them out from the land of Egypt. This is that night of the LORD, to be much observed of all the children of Yisra'el throughout their generations. The LORD said to Moshe and Aharon, "This is the ordinance of the Pesach. There shall no foreigner eat of it, but every man's servant who is bought for money, when you have circumcised him, then shall he eat of it. A foreigner and a hired servant shall not eat of it. In one house shall it be eaten; you shall not carry forth anything of the flesh abroad out of the house; neither shall you break a bone of it. All the congregation of Yisra'el shall keep it. When a stranger shall live as a foreigner with you, and will keep the Pesach to the LORD, let all his males be circumcised, and then let him come near and keep it; and he shall be as one who is born in the land: but no uncircumcised person shall eat of it. One law shall be to him who is born at home, and to the stranger who lives as a foreigner among you." Thus did all the children of Yisra'el. As the LORD commanded Moshe and Aharon, so they did. It happened the same day, that the LORD brought the children of Yisra'el out of the land of Egypt by their armies. The LORD spoke to Moshe, saying, "Sanctify to Me all of the firstborn, whatever opens the womb among the children of Yisra'el, both of man and of animal. It is Mine."

Haftarah

Jeremiah 46:25-26

The LORD of Armies, the God of Yisra'el, says: Behold, I will punish Amon of No, and Par'oh, and Egypt, with her gods, and her kings; even Par'oh, and those who trust in him: and I will deliver them into the hand of those who seek their lives, and into the hand of Nevukhadnetzar 1 king of Bavel, and into the hand of his servants; and afterwards it shall be inhabited, as in the days of old, says the LORD.

Brit Chadasha
John 19:1-37

Parashat Bo — Day 6

So Pilate then took Yeshua, and flogged Him. The soldiers twisted thorns into a crown, and put it on His head, and dressed Him in a purple garment. They kept saying, "Hail, King of the Jews!" and they kept slapping Him. Then Pilate went out again, and said to them, "Behold, I bring Him out to you, that you may know that I find no basis for a charge against Him." Yeshua therefore came out, wearing the crown of thorns and the purple garment. Pilate said to them, "Behold, the man!" When therefore the chief Kohanim and the officers saw Him, they shouted, saying, "Crucify! Crucify!" Now it was the Preparation Day of the Pesach, at about the sixth hour. He said to the Judeans, "Behold, your King!" They cried out, "Away with Him! Away with Him! Crucify Him!" Pilate said to them, "Shall I crucify your King?" The chief Kohanim answered, "We have no king but Caesar!" So then he delivered Him to them to be crucified. So they took Yeshua and led him away. He went out, bearing his cross, to the place called "The Place of a Skull," which is called in Hebrew, "Gulgolta," where they crucified Him, and with Him two others, on either side one, and Yeshua in the middle. Pilate wrote a title also, and put it on the cross.

There was written, "YESHUA OF NATZERET, THE KING OF THE JEWS." Then the soldiers, when they had crucified Yeshua, took His garments and made four parts, to every soldier a part; and also the coat. Now the coat was without seam, woven from the top throughout. Then they said to one another, "Let's not tear it, but cast lots for it to decide whose it will be," that the Scripture might be fulfilled, which says, "They parted my garments among them. For My cloak they cast lots." Therefore the soldiers did these things. After this, Yeshua, seeing that all things were now finished, that the Scripture might be fulfilled, said, "I am thirsty." Now a vessel full of vinegar was set there; so they put a sponge full of the vinegar on hyssop, and held it at His mouth. When Yeshua therefore had received the vinegar, He said, "It is finished." He bowed His head, and gave up His spirit. Therefore the Judeans, because it was the Preparation Day, so that the bodies wouldn't remain on the cross on the Shabbat (for that Shabbat was a special one), asked of Pilate that their legs might be broken, and that they might be taken away. Therefore the soldiers came, and broke the legs of the first, and of the other who was crucified with Him; but when they came to Yeshua, and saw that He was already dead, they didn't break His legs. However one of the soldiers pierced His side with a spear, and immediately blood and water came out. He who has seen has testified, and his testimony is true. He knows that he tells the truth, that you may believe. For these things happened, that the Scripture might be fulfilled, "A bone of Him will not be broken." Again another Scripture says, "They will look on Him whom they pierced."

Parashat: Bo - "Enter"

Daily Portion: Shabbat

Exodus 13:3-16

Moshe said to the people, "Remember this day, in which you came out from Egypt, out of the house of bondage; for by strength of hand the LORD brought you out from this place. No leavened bread shall be eaten.

This day you go forth in the month Aviv. It shall be, when the LORD shall bring you into the land of the Kena'ani, and the Chittite, and the Amori, and the Chivvi, and the Yevusi, which He swore to your fathers to give you, a land flowing with milk and honey, that you shall keep this service in this month.

Seven days you shall eat matzah, and in the seventh day shall be a feast to the LORD. Unleavened bread shall be eaten throughout the seven days; and no leavened bread shall be seen with you, neither shall there be yeast seen with you, in all your borders.

You shall tell your son in that day, saying, 'It is because of that which the LORD did for me when I came forth out of Egypt.' It shall be for a sign to you on your hand, and for a memorial between your eyes, that the law of the LORD may be in your mouth; for with a strong hand the LORD has brought you out of Egypt.

You shall therefore keep this ordinance in its season from year to year. "It shall be, when the LORD shall bring you into the land of the Kena`ani, as he swore to you and to your fathers, and shall give it you, that you shall set apart to the LORD all that opens the womb, and every firstborn which you have that comes from an animal.

The males shall be the LORD's. Every firstborn of a donkey you shall redeem with a lamb; and if you will not redeem it, then you shall break its neck; and you shall redeem all the firstborn of man among your sons.

It shall be, when your son asks you in time to come, saying, 'What is this?' that you shall tell him, 'By strength of hand the LORD brought us out from Egypt, from the house of bondage; and it happened, when Par'oh would hardly let us go, that the LORD killed all the firstborn in the land of Egypt, both the firstborn of man, and the firstborn of animal.

Therefore I sacrifice to the LORD all that opens the womb, being males; but all the firstborn of my sons I redeem.' It shall be for a sign on your hand, and for symbols between your eyes: for by strength of hand the LORD brought us forth out of Egypt."

Haftarah

Jeremiah 46:27-28

> Parashat Bo
> Day 7

But don't be afraid you, Ya'akov My servant, neither be dismayed, Yisra'el: for, behold, I will save you from afar, and your seed from the land of their captivity; and Ya'akov shall return, and shall be quiet and at ease, and none shall make him afraid.

Don't be afraid you, O Ya'akov My servant, says the LORD; for I am with you: for I will make a full end of all the nations where I have driven you; but I will not make a full end of you, but I will correct you in measure, and will in no way leave you unpunished.

Brit Chadasha

Luke 2:22-24

When the days of their purification according to the Torah of Moshe were fulfilled, they brought Him up to Yerushalayim, to present Him to the Lord (as it is written in the Torah of the Lord, "Every male who opens the womb shall be called holy to the Lord"), and to offer a sacrifice according to that which is said in the Torah of the Lord, "A pair of turtledoves, or two young pigeons."

Parashat: Beshalach - "When He Let Go"

Daily Portion: Sunday

Exodus 13:17-14:9

It happened, when Par'oh had let the people go, that God didn't lead them by the way of the land of the Pelishtim, although that was near; for God said, "Lest perhaps the people change their minds when they see war, and they return to Egypt;" but God led the people around by the way of the wilderness by the Sea of Suf; and the children of Yisra'el went up armed out of the land of Egypt.

Moshe took the bones of Yosef with him, for he had made the children of Yisra'el swear, saying, "God will surely visit you, and you shall carry up my bones away from here with you." They took their journey from Sukkot, and encamped in Etam, in the edge of the wilderness.

The LORD went before them by day in a pillar of cloud, to lead them on their way, and by night in a pillar of fire, to give them light, that they might go by day and by night: the pillar of cloud by day, and the pillar of fire by night, didn't depart from before the people.

The LORD spoke to Moshe, saying, "Speak to the children of Yisra'el, that they turn back and encamp before Pi-Hachirot, between Migdol and the sea, before Ba`al-Tzefon. You shall encamp opposite it by the sea.

Par'oh will say of the children of Yisra'el, 'They are entangled in the land. The wilderness has shut them in.' I will harden Par'oh's heart, and he will follow after them; and I will get honor over Par'oh, and over all his armies; and the Egyptians shall know that I am the LORD."

They did so. It was told the king of Egypt that the people had fled; and the heart of Par'oh and of his servants was changed towards the people, and they said, "What is this we have done, that we have let Yisra'el go from serving us?"

He made ready his chariot, and took his army with him; and he took six hundred chosen chariots, and all the chariots of Egypt, and captains over all of them.

The LORD hardened the heart of Par'oh king of Egypt, and he pursued after the children of Yisra'el; for the children of Yisra'el went out with a high hand.

The Egyptians pursued after them: all the horses and chariots of Par'oh, his horsemen, and his army; and overtook them encamping by the sea, beside Pi-Hachirot, before Ba'al-Tzefon.

Haftarah

Judges 4:4-9

Now Devorah, a prophetess, the wife of Lappidot, she judged Yisra'el at that time. She lived under the palm tree of Devorah between Ramah and Beit-El in the hill country of Efrayim: and the children of Yisra'el came up to her for judgment.

She sent and called Barak the son of Avino'am out of Kedesh-Naftali, and said to him, Hasn't the LORD, the God of Yisra'el, commanded, [saying], Go and draw to Mount Tavor, and take with you ten thousand men of the children of Naftali and of the children of Zevulun?

I will draw to you, to the river Kishon, Sisera, the captain of Yavin's army, with his chariots and his multitude; and I will deliver him into your hand. Barak said to her, If you will go with me, then I will go; but if you will not go with me, I will not go. She said, I will surely go with you: notwithstanding, the journey that you take shall not be for your honor; for the LORD will sell Sisera into the hand of a woman. Devorah arose, and went with Barak to Kedesh.

Parashat Beshalach — Day 1

Brit Chadasha

Hebrews 11:22-29

By faith, Yosef, when his end was near, made mention of the departure of the children of Yisra'el; and gave instructions concerning his bones.

By faith, Moshe, when he was born, was hidden for three months by his parents, because they saw that he was a beautiful child, and they were not afraid of the king's mitzvah.

By faith, Moshe, when he had grown up, refused to be called the son of Par'oh's daughter, choosing rather to share ill treatment with God's people, than to enjoy the pleasures of sin for a time; accounting the reproach of Messiah greater riches than the treasures of Egypt; for he looked to the reward.

By faith, he left Egypt, not fearing the wrath of the king; for he endured, as seeing him who is invisible.

By faith, he kept the Pesach, and the sprinkling of the blood, that the destroyer of the firstborn should not touch them.

Parashat: Beshalach - "When He Let Go"

Daily Portion: Monday

Exodus 14:10-25

When Par'oh drew near, the children of Yisra'el lifted up their eyes, and behold, the Egyptians were marching after them; and they were very afraid. The children of Yisra'el cried out to the LORD. They said to Moshe, "Because there were no graves in Egypt, have you taken us away to die in the wilderness? Why have you treated us this way, to bring us forth out of Egypt? Isn't this the word that we spoke to you in Egypt, saying, 'Leave us alone, that we may serve the Egyptians?' For it were better for us to serve the Egyptians, than that we should die in the wilderness." Moshe said to the people, "Don't be afraid. Stand still, and see the salvation of the LORD, which He will work for you today: for the Egyptians whom you have seen today, you shall never see them again. The LORD will fight for you, and you shall be still." The LORD said to Moshe, "Why do you cry to Me? Speak to the children of Yisra'el, that they go forward. Lift up your rod, and stretch out your hand over the sea, and divide it: and the children of Yisra'el shall go into the midst of the sea on dry ground. I, behold, I will harden the hearts of the Egyptians, and they shall go in after them: and I will get Myself honor over Par'oh, and over all his armies, over his chariots, and over his horsemen. The Egyptians shall know that I am the LORD, when I have gotten Myself honor over Par'oh, over his chariots, and over his horsemen." The angel of God, who went before the camp of Yisra'el, moved and went behind them; and the pillar of cloud moved from before them, and stood behind them. It came between the camp of Egypt and the camp of Yisra'el; and there was the cloud and the darkness, yet gave it light by night: and the one didn't come near the other all the night. Moshe stretched out his hand over the sea, and the LORD caused the sea to go back by a strong east wind all the night, and made the sea dry land, and the waters were divided. The children of Yisra'el went into the midst of the sea on the dry ground, and the waters were a wall to them on their right hand, and on their left. The Egyptians pursued, and went in after them into the midst of the sea: all of Par'oh's horses, his chariots, and his horsemen. It happened in the morning watch, that the LORD looked out on the Egyptian army through the pillar of fire and of cloud, and confused the Egyptian army. He took off their chariot wheels, and they drove them heavily; so that the Egyptians said, "Let's flee from the face of Yisra'el, for the LORD fights for them against the Egyptians!"

Haftarah

Judges 4:10-17

Barak called Zevulun and Naftali together to Kedesh; and there went up ten thousand men at his feet: and Devorah went up with him. Now Chever the Keni had separated himself from the Kinim, even from the children of Chovav the brother-in-law of Moshe, and had pitched his tent as far as the oak in Tza'anannim, which is by Kedesh. They told Sisera that Barak the son of Avino'am was gone up to Mount Tavor. Sisera gathered together all his chariots, even nine hundred chariots of iron, and all the people who were with him, from Charoshet of the Gentiles, to the river Kishon. Devorah said to Barak, Up;

for this is the day in which the LORD has delivered Sisera into your hand; hasn't the LORD gone out before you? So Barak went down from Mount Tavor, and ten thousand men after him. The LORD confused Sisera, and all his chariots, and all his army, with the edge of the sword before Barak; and Sisera alighted from his chariot, and fled away on his feet. But Barak pursued after the chariots, and after the army, to Charoshet of the Gentiles: and all the army of Sisera fell by the edge of the sword; there was not a man left. However Sisera fled away on his feet to the tent of Ya'el the wife of Chever the Keni; for there was shalom between Yavin the king of Chatzor and the house of Chever the Keni.

Parashat Beshalach Day 2

Brit Chadasha

Romans 6:1-23

What shall we say then? Shall we continue in sin, that grace may abound? May it never be! We who died to sin, how could we live in it any longer? Or don't you know that all we who were immersed into Messiah Yeshua were immersed into His death? We were buried therefore with Him through immersion to death, that just like Messiah was raised from the dead through the glory of the Father, so we also might walk in newness of life.

For if we have become united with Him in the likeness of His death, we will also be part of His resurrection; knowing this, that our old man was crucified with Him, that the body of sin might be done away with, so that we would no longer be in bondage to sin. For he who has died has been freed from sin. But if we died with Messiah, we believe that we will also live with Him; knowing that Messiah, being raised from the dead, dies no more. Death no more has dominion over Him! For the death that He died, He died to sin one time; but the life that He lives, He lives to God. Thus also consider yourselves also to be dead to sin, but alive to God in Messiah Yeshua our Lord.

Therefore don't let sin reign in your mortal body, that you should obey it in its lusts. Neither present your members to sin as instruments of unrighteousness, but present yourselves to God, as alive from the dead, and your members as instruments of righteousness to God. For sin will not have dominion over you. For you are not under law, but under grace. What then? Shall we sin, because we are not under law, but under grace? May it never be! Don't you know that to whom you present yourselves as servants to obedience, his servants you are whom you obey; whether of sin to death, or of obedience to righteousness? But thanks be to God, that, whereas you were bondservants of sin, you became obedient from the heart to that form of teaching whereunto you were delivered. Being made free from sin, you became bondservants of righteousness.

I speak in human terms because of the weakness of your flesh, for as you presented your members as servants to uncleanness and to wickedness upon wickedness, even so now present your members as servants to righteousness for sanctification. For when you were servants of sin, you were free in regard to righteousness. What fruit then did you have at that time in the things of which you are now ashamed? For the end of those things is death. But now, being made free from sin, and having become servants of God, you have your fruit of sanctification, and the result of eternal life. For the wages of sin is death, but the free gift of God is eternal life in Messiah Yeshua our Lord.

Parashat: Beshalach - "When He Let Go"

Daily Portion: Tuesday

Exodus 14:26-15:13

The LORD said to Moshe, "Stretch out your hand over the sea, that the waters may come again on the Egyptians, on their chariots, and on their horsemen." Moshe stretched out his hand over the sea, and the sea returned to its strength when the morning appeared; and the Egyptians fled against it. The LORD overthrew the Egyptians in the midst of the sea. The waters returned, and covered the chariots and the horsemen, even all Par'oh's army that went in after them into the sea.

There remained not so much as one of them. But the children of Yisra'el walked on dry land in the midst of the sea, and the waters were a wall to them on their right hand, and on their left. Thus the LORD saved Yisra'el that day out of the hand of the Egyptians; and Yisra'el saw the Egyptians dead on the seashore. Yisra'el saw the great work which the LORD did to the Egyptians, and the people feared the LORD; and they believed in the LORD, and in His servant Moshe.

Then Moshe and the children of Yisra'el sang this song to the LORD, and said, "I will sing to the LORD, for He has triumphed gloriously. The horse and his rider He has thrown into the sea. The LORD is my strength and song. He has become my yeshu'ah. This is my God, and I will praise Him; my father's God, and I will exalt Him. The LORD is a man of war. The LORD is His name. He has cast Par'oh's chariots and his army into the sea. His chosen captains are sunk in the Sea of Suf. The deeps cover them. They went down into the depths like a stone.

Your right hand, LORD, is glorious in power. Your right hand, LORD, dashes the enemy in pieces. In the greatness of Your excellency, You overthrow those who rise up against You. You send forth Your wrath. It consumes them as stubble. With the blast of Your nostrils, the waters were piled up. The floods stood upright as a heap. The deeps were congealed in the heart of the sea. The enemy said, 'I will pursue. I will overtake. I will divide the spoil. My desire shall be satisfied on them. I will draw my sword, my hand shall destroy them.' You blew with Your wind. The sea covered them. They sank like lead in the mighty waters.

Who is like You, LORD, among the gods? Who is like You, glorious in holiness, fearful in praises, doing wonders? You stretched out Your right hand. The earth swallowed them. "You, in Your loving kindness, have led the people that You have redeemed. You have guided them in Your strength to Your holy habitation.

Haftarah

Judges 4:18-23

Parashat Beshalach — Day 3

Ya'el went out to meet Sisera, and said to him, Turn in, my lord, turn in to me; don't be afraid. He came in to her into the tent, and she covered him with a rug. He said to her, Please give me a little water to drink; for I am thirsty.

She opened a bottle of milk, and gave him drink, and covered him. He said to her, Stand in the door of the tent, and it shall be, when any man does come and inquire of you, and say, Is there any man here? that you shall say, No.

Then Ya'el Chever's wife took a tent peg, and took a hammer in her hand, and went softly to him, and struck the pin into his temples, and it pierced through into the ground; for he was in a deep sleep; so he swooned and died.

Behold, as Barak pursued Sisera, Ya'el came out to meet him, and said to him, Come, and I will show you the man whom you seek.

He came to her; and behold, Sisera lay dead, and the tent peg was in his temples. So God subdued on that day Yavin the king of Kena'an before the children of Yisra'el.

Brit Chadasha

Revelation 15:1-4

I saw another great and marvelous sign in the sky: seven angels having the seven last plagues, for in them God's wrath is finished. I saw something like a sea of glass mixed with fire, and those who overcame the beast, his image, and the number of his name, standing on the sea of glass, having harps of God.

They sang the song of Moshe, the servant of God, and the song of the Lamb, saying, "Great and marvelous are Your works, Lord God, the Almighty! Righteous and true are Your ways, You King of the nations.

Who wouldn't fear You, Lord, and glorify Your name? For You only are holy. For all the nations will come and worship before You. For Your righteous acts have been revealed."

Parashat: Beshalach - "When He Let Go"

Daily Portion: Wednesday

Exodus 15:14-16:1

The peoples have heard. They tremble. Pangs have taken hold on the inhabitants of Pelesheth. Then the chiefs of Edom were dismayed. Trembling takes hold of the mighty men of Mo'av. All the inhabitants of Kena'an are melted away. Terror and dread falls on them. By the greatness of Your arm they are as still as a stone— until Your people pass over, LORD, until the people pass over who You have purchased. You shall bring them in, and plant them in the mountain of Your inheritance, the place, LORD, which You have made for Yourself to dwell in; the sanctuary, Lord, which Your hands have established. The LORD shall reign forever and ever." For the horses of Par'oh went in with his chariots and with his horsemen into the sea, and the LORD brought back the waters of the sea on them; but the children of Yisra'el walked on dry land in the midst of the sea.

Miryam the prophetess, the sister of Aharon, took a tambourine in her hand; and all the women went out after her with timbrels and with dances. Miryam answered them, "Sing to the LORD, for He has triumphed gloriously. The horse and his rider He has thrown into the sea." Moshe led Yisra'el onward from the Sea of Suf, and they went out into the wilderness of Shur; and they went three days in the wilderness, and found no water. When they came to Marah, they couldn't drink from the waters of Marah, for they were bitter. Therefore the name of it was called Marah. The people murmured against Moshe, saying, "What shall we drink?" Then he cried to the LORD. The LORD showed him a tree, and he threw it into the waters, and the waters were made sweet.

There He made a statute and an ordinance for them, and there He tested them; and He said, "If you will diligently listen to the voice of the LORD your God, and will do that which is right in His eyes, and will pay attention to His mitzvot, and keep all His statutes, I will put none of the diseases on you, which I have put on the Egyptians; for I am the LORD who heals you." They came to Elim, where there were twelve springs of water, and seventy palm trees: and they encamped there by the waters. They took their journey from Elim, and all the congregation of the children of Yisra'el came to the wilderness of Sin, which is between Elim and Sinai, on the fifteenth day of the second month after their departing out of the land of Egypt.

Haftarah

Judges 4:24-5:8

The hand of the children of Yisra'el prevailed more and more against Yavin the king of Kena'an, until they had destroyed Yavin king of Kena'an. Then Devorah and Barak the son of Avino'am sang on that day, saying, Because the leaders took the lead in Yisra'el, because the people offered themselves willingly, be blessed, the LORD! Hear, you kings! Give ear, you princes! I, [even] I, will sing to the LORD.

Parashat Beshalach Day 4

I will sing praise to the LORD, the God of Yisra'el. LORD, when you went forth out of Se'ir, when you marched out of the field of Edom, the earth trembled, the sky also dropped. Yes, the clouds dropped water. The mountains quaked at the presence of the LORD, even Sinai, at the presence of the LORD, the God of Yisra'el. In the days of Shamgar the son of 'Anat, in the days of Ya'el, the highways were unoccupied. The travelers walked through byways. The rulers ceased in Yisra'el. They ceased until I, Devorah, arose; Until I arose a mother in Yisra'el. They chose new gods. Then war was in the gates. Was there a shield or spear seen among forty thousand in Yisra'el?

Brit Chadasha

1Corinthians 10:1-13

Now I would not have you ignorant, brothers, that our fathers were all under the cloud, and all passed through the sea; and were all immersed into Moshe in the cloud and in the sea; and all ate the same spiritual food; and all drank the same spiritual drink. For they drank of a spiritual rock that followed them, and the rock was Messiah. However with most of them, God was not well pleased, for they were overthrown in the wilderness. Now these things were our examples, to the intent we should not lust after evil things, as they also lusted. Neither be idolaters, as some of them were.

As it is written, "The people sat down to eat and drink, and rose up to play." Neither let us commit sexual immorality, as some of them committed, and in one day twenty-three thousand fell. Neither let us test the Lord, as some of them tested, and perished by the serpents. Neither grumble, as some of them also grumbled, and perished by the destroyer. Now all these things happened to them by way of example, and they were written for our admonition, on whom the ends of the ages have come. Therefore let him who thinks he stands be careful that he doesn't fall. No temptation has taken you except what is common to man. God is faithful, who will not allow you to be tempted above what you are able, but will with the temptation also make the way of escape, that you may be able to endure it.

Parashat: Beshalach - "When He Let Go"

Daily Portion: Thursday

Exodus 16:2-15

The whole congregation of the children of Yisra'el murmured against Moshe and against Aharon in the wilderness; and the children of Yisra'el said to them, "We wish that we had died by the hand of the LORD in the land of Egypt, when we sat by the meat pots, when we ate our fill of bread, for you have brought us out into this wilderness, to kill this whole assembly with hunger." Then said the LORD to Moshe, "Behold, I will rain bread from the sky for you, and the people shall go out and gather a day's portion every day, that I may test them, whether they will walk in My law, or not. It shall come to pass on the sixth day, that they shall prepare that which they bring in, and it shall be twice as much as they gather daily." Moshe and Aharon said to all the children of Yisra'el, "At evening, then you shall know that the LORD has brought you out from the land of Egypt; and in the morning, then you shall see the glory of the LORD; because He hears your murmurings against the LORD. Who are we, that you murmur against us?" Moshe said, "Now the LORD shall give you meat to eat in the evening, and in the morning bread to satisfy you; because the LORD hears your murmurings which you murmur against Him.

And who are we? Your murmurings are not against us, but against the LORD." Moshe said to Aharon, "Tell all the congregation of the children of Yisra'el, 'Come near before the LORD, for He has heard your murmurings.'" It happened, as Aharon spoke to the whole congregation of the children of Yisra'el, that they looked toward the wilderness, and behold, the glory of the LORD appeared in the cloud. The LORD spoke to Moshe, saying, "I have heard the murmurings of the children of Yisra'el. Speak to them, saying, 'At evening you shall eat meat, and in the morning you shall be filled with bread: and you shall know that I am the LORD your God.'" It happened at evening that quail came up and covered the camp; and in the morning the dew lay around the camp. When the dew that lay had gone, behold, on the surface of the wilderness was a small round thing, small as the frost on the ground. When the children of Yisra'el saw it, they said one to another, "What is it?" For they didn't know what it was. Moshe said to them, "It is the bread which the LORD has given you to eat."

Haftarah

Judges 5:9-16

My heart is toward the governors of Yisra'el, who offered themselves willingly among the people. Bless the LORD! Tell [of it], you who ride on white donkeys, you who sit on rich carpets, and you who walk by the way. Far from the noise of archers, in the places of drawing water, there they will rehearse the righteous acts of the LORD, [Even] the righteous acts of his rule in Yisra'el. Then the people of the LORD went down to the gates. Awake, awake, Devorah! Awake, awake, utter a song!

Parashat Beshalach Day 5

Arise, Barak, and lead away your captives, you son of Avino'am.
Then a remnant of the nobles [and] the people came down. The LORD came down for me against the mighty. Those whose root is in 'Amalek came out of Efrayim, after you, Binyamin, among your peoples. Governors come down out of Makhir. Those who handle the marshal's staff came out of Zevulun. The princes of Yissakhar were with Devorah. As was Yissakhar, so was Barak. They rushed into the valley at his feet. By the watercourses of Re'uven, there were great resolves of heart. Why did you sit among the sheepfolds, To hear the whistling for the flocks? At the watercourses of Re'uven There were great searchings of heart.

Brit Chadasha

John 6:25-35

When they found Him on the other side of the sea, they asked Him, "Rabbi, when did You come here?" Yeshua answered them, "Most certainly I tell you, you seek Me, not because you saw signs, but because you ate of the loaves, and were filled. Don't work for the food which perishes, but for the food which remains to eternal life, which the Son of Man will give to you. For God the Father has sealed Him."

They said therefore to Him, "What must we do, that we may work the works of God?" Yeshua answered them, "This is the work of God, that you believe in Him whom He has sent." They said therefore to Him, "What then do You do for a sign, that we may see, and believe You? What work do You do? Our fathers ate the manna in the wilderness. As it is written, 'He gave them bread out of heaven to eat.'"

Yeshua therefore said to them, "Most certainly, I tell you, it wasn't Moshe who gave you the bread out of heaven, but My Father gives you the true bread out of heaven. For the bread of God is that which comes down out of heaven, and gives life to the world." They said therefore to him, "Lord, always give us this bread." Yeshua said to them, "I am the bread of life. He who comes to Me will not be hungry, and he who believes in Me will never be thirsty.

Parashat Beshalach

Day 6

Parashat: Beshalach - "When He Let Go"

Daily Portion: Friday

Exodus 16:16-34

This is the thing which the LORD has commanded: "Gather of it everyone according to his eating; an omer a head, according to the number of your persons, shall you take it, every man for those who are in his tent." The children of Yisra'el did so, and gathered some more, some less. When they measured it with an omer, he who gathered much had nothing over, and he who gathered little had no lack. They gathered every man according to his eating. Moshe said to them, "Let no one leave of it until the morning." Notwithstanding they didn't listen to Moshe, but some of them left of it until the morning, and it bred worms, and became foul: and Moshe was angry with them. They gathered it morning by morning, everyone according to his eating. When the sun grew hot, it melted. It happened that on the sixth day they gathered twice as much bread, two omers for each one, and all the rulers of the congregation came and told Moshe. He said to them, "This is that which the LORD has spoken, 'Tomorrow is a solemn rest, a holy Shabbat to the LORD. Bake that which you want to bake, and boil that which you want to boil; and all that remains over lay up for yourselves to be kept until the morning.'" They laid it up until the morning, as Moshe asked, and it didn't become foul, neither was there any worm in it. Moshe said, "Eat that today, for today is a Shabbat to the LORD. Today you shall not find it in the field. Six days you shall gather it, but on the seventh day is the Shabbat. In it there shall be none." It happened on the seventh day, that some of the people went out to gather, and they found none. The LORD said to Moshe, "How long do you refuse to keep My mitzvot and My laws? Behold, because the LORD has given you the Shabbat, therefore He gives you on the sixth day the bread of two days. Everyone stay in his place. Let no one go out of his place on the seventh day." So the people rested on the seventh day. The house of Yisra'el called the name of it Manna, and it was like coriander seed, white; and its taste was like wafers with honey. Moshe said, "This is the thing which the LORD has commanded, 'Let an omer full of it be kept throughout your generations, that they may see the bread with which I fed you in the wilderness, when I brought you forth from the land of Egypt.'" Moshe said to Aharon, "Take a pot, and put an omer-full of manna in it, and lay it up before the LORD, to be kept throughout your generations." As the LORD commanded Moshe, so Aharon laid it up before the Testimony, to be kept.

Haftarah

Judges 5:17-23

Gil'ad lived beyond the Yarden. Why did Dan remain in ships? Asher sat still at the haven of the sea, and lived by his creeks. Zevulun was a people that jeopardized their lives to the deaths; Naftali also, on the high places of the field. The kings came and fought, then the kings of Kena'an fought at Ta'nakh by the waters of Megiddo. They took no plunder of silver. From the sky the stars fought. From their courses, they fought against Sisera. The river Kishon swept them away, that ancient river, the river Kishon. My soul, march on with strength. Then the horse hoofs stamped becaus of the prancings, the prancings of their strong ones. Curse Meroz, said the angel of the LORD. Curse bitterly its inhabitants, because they didn't come to help the LORD, to help the LORD against the mighty.

Parashat Beshalach Day 6

Brit Chadasha

2Corinthians 8:1-15

Moreover, brothers, we make known to you the grace of God which has been given in the assemblies of Macedonia; how that in much proof of affliction the abundance of their joy and their deep poverty abounded to the riches of their liberality. For according to their power, I testify, yes and beyond their power, they gave of their own accord, begging us with much entreaty to receive this grace and the fellowship in the service to the holy ones. This was not as we had hoped, but first they gave their own selves to the Lord, and to us through the will of God. So we urged Titus, that as he made a beginning before, so he would also complete in you this grace. But as you abound in everything, in faith, utterance, knowledge, all earnestness, and in your love to us, see that you also abound in this grace. I speak not by way of mitzvah, but as proving through the earnestness of others the sincerity also of your love.

For you know the grace of our Lord Yeshua the Messiah, that, though He was rich, yet for your sakes He became poor, that you through His poverty might become rich. I give a judgment in this: for this is expedient for you, who were the first to start a year ago, not only to do, but also to be willing. But now complete the doing also, that as there was the readiness to be willing, so there may be the completion also out of your ability. For if the readiness is there, it is acceptable according to what you have, not according to what you don't have. For this is not that others may be eased and you distressed, but for equality. Your abundance at this present time supplies their lack, that their abundance also may become a supply for your lack; that there may be equality. As it is written, "He who gathered much had nothing left over, and he who gathered little had no lack."

Parashat: Beshalach - "When He Let Go"

Daily Portion: Shabbat

Exodus 16:35-17:16

The children of Yisra'el ate the manna forty years, until they came to an inhabited land. They ate the manna until they came to the borders of the land of Kena'an. Now an omer is the tenth part of an efah. All the congregation of the children of Yisra'el traveled from the wilderness of Sin, by their journeys, according to the LORD's mitzvah, and encamped in Refidim; but there was no water for the people to drink.

Therefore the people quarreled with Moshe, and said, "Give us water to drink." Moshe said to them, "Why do you quarrel with me? Why do you test the LORD?" The people were thirsty for water there; and the people murmured against Moshe, and said, "Why have you brought us up out of Egypt, to kill us, our children, and our livestock with thirst?" Moshe cried to the LORD, saying, "What shall I do with these people? They are almost ready to stone me."

The LORD said to Moshe, "Walk on before the people, and take the elders of Yisra'el with you, and take the rod in your hand with which you struck the Nile, and go. Behold, I will stand before you there on the rock in Chorev. You shall strike the rock, and water will come out of it, that the people may drink." Moshe did so in the sight of the elders of Yisra'el. He called the name of the place Massah, and Merivah, because the children of Yisra'el quarreled, and because they tested the LORD, saying, "Is the LORD among us, or not?"

Then 'Amalek came and fought with Yisra'el in Refidim. Moshe said to Yehoshua, "Choose men for us, and go out, fight with `Amalek. Tomorrow I will stand on the top of the hill with God's rod in my hand." So Yehoshua did as Moshe had told him, and fought with 'Amalek; and Moshe, Aharon, and Chur went up to the top of the hill. It happened, when Moshe held up his hand, that Yisra'el prevailed; and when he let down his hand, 'Amalek prevailed.

But Moshe' hands were heavy; and they took a stone, and put it under him, and he sat on it. Aharon and Chur held up his hands, the one on the one side, and the other on the other side. His hands were steady until sunset. Yehoshua defeated 'Amalek and his people with the edge of the sword.

The LORD said to Moshe, "Write this for a memorial in a book, and rehearse it in the ears of Yehoshua: that I will utterly blot out the memory of `Amalek from under the sky." Moshe built an altar, and called the name of it the LORD our Banner. He said, "The LORD has sworn: 'The LORD will have war with `Amalek from generation to generation.'"

Haftarah

Judges 5:24-30

> Parashat Beshalach
> Day 7

Ya'el shall be blessed above women, the wife of Chever the Keni; blessed shall she be above women in the tent. He asked for water. She gave him milk. She brought him butter in a lordly dish. She put her hand to the tent peg, and her right hand to the workmen's hammer. With the hammer she struck Sisera. She struck through his head. Yes, she pierced and struck through his temples. At her feet he bowed, he fell, he lay. At her feet he bowed, he fell. Where he bowed, there he fell down dead. Through the window she looked out, and cried: Sisera's mother looked through the lattice. Why is his chariot so long in coming? Why do the wheels of his chariots wait? Her wise ladies answered her, Yes, she returned answer to herself, Have they not found, have they not divided the spoil? A lady, two ladies to every man; to Sisera a spoil of dyed garments, A spoil of dyed garments embroidered, Of dyed garments embroidered on both sides, on the necks of the spoil?

Brit Chadasha

John 7:26-38

Behold, He speaks openly, and they say nothing to Him. Can it be that the rulers indeed know that this is truly the Messiah? However we know where this man comes from, but when the Messiah comes, no one will know where He comes from." Yeshua therefore cried out in the temple, teaching and saying, "You both know Me, and know where I am from. I have not come of Myself, but He who sent Me is true, whom you don't know. I know Him, because I am from Him, and He sent Me." They sought therefore to take Him; but no one laid a hand on Him, because His hour had not yet come. But of the multitude, many believed in Him. They said, "When the Messiah comes, He won't do more signs than those which this man has done, will He?" The Perushim heard the multitude murmuring these things concerning Him, and the chief Kohanim and the Perushim sent officers to arrest Him. Then Yeshua said, "I will be with you a little while longer, then I go to Him who sent Me. You will seek Me, and won't find Me; and where I am, you can't come." The Judeans therefore said among themselves, "Where will this man go that we won't find Him? Will He go to the Diaspora among the Greeks, and teach the Greeks? What is this word that He said, 'You will seek Me, and won't find Me; and where I am, you can't come'?" Now on the last day of the feast, Hoshana Rabbah, Yeshua stood and cried out, "If anyone is thirsty, let Him come to Me and drink! He who believes in Me, as the Scripture has said, from within him will flow rivers of living water."

Parashat: Yitro - "Jethro"

Daily Portion: Sunday

Exodus 18:1-12

Now Yitro, the Kohen of Midyan, Moshe' father-in-law, heard of all that God had done for Moshe, and for Yisra'el his people, how that the LORD had brought Yisra'el out of Egypt. Yitro, Moshe' father-in-law, received Tzipporah, Moshe' wife, after he had sent her away, and her two sons.

The name of one son was Gershom, for Moshe said, "I have lived as a foreigner in a foreign land". The name of the other was Eli'ezer, for he said, "My father's God was my help and delivered me from Par'oh's sword." Yitro, Moshe' father-in-law, came with his sons and his wife to Moshe into the wilderness where he was encamped, at the Mountain of God.

He said to Moshe, I, your father-in-law Yitro, have come to you with your wife, and her two sons with her. Moshe went out to meet his father-in-law, and bowed and kissed him. They asked each other of their welfare, and they came into the tent. Moshe told his father-in-law all that the LORD had done to Par'oh and to the Egyptians for Yisra'el's sake, all the hardships that had come on them on the way, and how the LORD delivered them.

Yitro rejoiced for all the goodness which the LORD had done to Yisra'el, in that He had delivered them out of the hand of the Egyptians. Yitro said, "Blessed be the LORD, who has delivered you out of the hand of the Egyptians, and out of the hand of Par`oh; who has delivered the people from under the hand of the Egyptians.

Now I know that the LORD is greater than all gods because of the thing in which they dealt arrogantly against them." Yitro, Moshe' father-in-law, took a burnt offering and sacrifices for God. Aharon came with all of the elders of Yisra'el, to eat bread with Moshe' father-in-law before God.

Haftarah

Isaiah 6:1-4

In the year that king 'Uzziyah died, I saw the Lord sitting on a throne, high and lifted up; and His train filled the temple. Above Him stood the serafim. Each one had six wings. With two he covered his face. With two he covered his feet. With two he flew. One called to another, and said, "Holy, holy, holy, is the LORD of

Armies! The whole earth is full of His glory!" The foundations of the thresholds shook at the voice of him who called, and the house was filled with smoke.

Parashat Yitro — Day 1

Brit Chadasha

Matthew 5:1-20

Seeing the multitudes, He went up onto the mountain. When He had sat down, His talmidim came to Him. He opened His mouth and taught them, saying, "Blessed are the poor in spirit, for theirs is the Kingdom of Heaven.

Blessed are those who mourn, for they shall be comforted. Blessed are the gentle, for they shall inherit the earth. Blessed are those who hunger and thirst after righteousness, for they shall be filled. Blessed are the merciful, for they shall obtain mercy.

Blessed are the pure in heart, for they shall see God. Blessed are the peacemakers, for they shall be called children of God. Blessed are those who have been persecuted for righteousness' sake, for theirs is the Kingdom of Heaven. "Blessed are you when people reproach you, persecute you, and say all kinds of evil against you falsely, for My sake.

Rejoice, and be exceedingly glad, for great is your reward in heaven. For that is how they persecuted the prophets who were before you. "You are the salt of the earth, but if the salt has lost its flavor, with what will it be salted? It is then good for nothing, but to be cast out and trodden under the feet of men.

You are the light of the world. A city located on a hill can't be hidden. Neither do you light a lamp, and put it under a measuring basket, but on a stand; and it shines to all who are in the house. Even so, let your light shine before men; that they may see your good works, and glorify your Father who is in heaven.

"Don't think that I came to destroy the Torah or the Prophets. I didn't come to destroy, but to fulfill. For most certainly, I tell you, until heaven and earth pass away, not even one smallest letter or one tiny pen stroke shall in any way pass away from the Torah, until all things are accomplished. Whoever, therefore, shall break one of these least mitzvot, and teach others to do so, shall be called least in the Kingdom of Heaven; but whoever shall do and teach them shall be called great in the Kingdom of Heaven.

For I tell you that unless your righteousness exceeds that of the scribes and Perushim, there is no way you will enter into the Kingdom of Heaven.

Parashat: Yitro - "Jethro"

Daily Portion: Monday

Exodus 18:13-23

It happened on the next day, that Moshe sat to judge the people, and the people stood around Moshe from the morning to the evening. When Moshe' father-in-law saw all that he did to the people, he said, "What is this thing that you do for the people? Why do you sit alone, and all the people stand around you from morning to evening?"

Moshe said to his father-in-law, "Because the people come to me to inquire of God. When they have a matter, they come to me, and I judge between a man and his neighbor, and I make them know the statutes of God, and His laws."

Moshe' father-in-law said to him, "The thing that you do is not good. You will surely wear away, both you, and this people that is with you; for the thing is too heavy for you. You are not able to perform it yourself alone. Listen now to my voice.

I will give you counsel, and God be with you. You represent the people before God, and bring the causes to God. You shall teach them the statutes and the laws, and shall show them the way in which they must walk, and the work that they must do. Moreover you shall provide out of all the people able men, such as fear God: men of truth, hating unjust gain; and place such over them, to be rulers of thousands, rulers of hundreds, rulers of fifties, and rulers of tens.

Let them judge the people at all times. It shall be that every great matter they shall bring to you, but every small matter they shall judge themselves. So shall it be easier for you, and they shall share the load with you. If you will do this thing, and God commands you so, then you will be able to endure, and all of these people also will go to their place in shalom."

Haftarah

Isaiah 6:5-8

Then I said, "Woe is me! For I am undone, because I am a man of unclean lips, and I dwell in the midst of a people of unclean lips: for my eyes have seen the King, the LORD of Armies!"

Then one of the serafim flew to me, having a live coal in his hand, which he had taken with the tongs from off the altar. He touched my mouth with it, and said,

"Behold, this has touched your lips; and your iniquity is taken away, and your sin forgiven."

I heard the Lord's voice, saying, "Whom shall I send, and who will go for Us?" Then I said, "Here I am. Send me!"

Parashat Yitro

Day 2

Brit Chadasha

Matthew 19:16-30

Behold, one came to Him and said, "Good teacher, what good thing shall I do, that I may have eternal life?" He said to him, "Why do you call Me good? No one is good but One, that is, God.

But if you want to enter into life, keep the mitzvot." He said to Him, "Which ones?" Yeshua said, "'You shall not murder.' 'You shall not commit adultery.' 'You shall not steal.' 'You shall not offer false testimony.' 'Honor your father and mother.' And, 'You shall love your neighbor as yourself.'"

The young man said to Him, "All these things I have observed from my youth. What do I still lack?" Yeshua said to him, "If you want to be perfect, go, sell what you have, and give to the poor, and you will have treasure in heaven; and come, follow Me."

But when the young man heard the saying, he went away sad, for he was one who had great possessions. Yeshua said to His talmidim, "Most certainly I say to you, a rich man will enter into the Kingdom of Heaven with difficulty.

Again I tell you, it is easier for a camel to go through a needle's eye, than for a rich man to enter into the Kingdom of God." When the talmidim heard it, they were exceedingly astonished, saying, "Who then can be saved?"

Looking at them, Yeshua said, "With men this is impossible, but with God all things are possible." Then Kefa answered, "Behold, we have left everything, and followed You. What then will we have?"

Yeshua said to them, "Most certainly I tell you that you who have followed Me, in the regeneration when the Son of Man will sit on the throne of His glory, you also will sit on twelve thrones, judging the twelve tribes of Yisra'el.

Everyone who has left houses, or brothers, or sisters, or father, or mother, or wife, or children, or lands, for My name's sake, will receive one hundred times, and will inherit eternal life. But many will be last who are first; and first who are last.

Parashat: Yitro - "Jethro"

Daily Portion: Tuesday

Exodus 18:24-19:8

So Moshe listened to the voice of his father-in-law, and did all that he had said. Moshe chose able men out of all Yisra'el, and made them heads over the people, rulers of thousands, rulers of hundreds, rulers of fifties, and rulers of tens. They judged the people at all times. They brought the hard causes to Moshe, but every small matter they judged themselves. Moshe let his father-in-law depart, and he went his way into his own land. In the third month after the children of Yisra'el had gone forth out of the land of Egypt, on that same day they came into the wilderness of Sinai. When they had departed from Refidim, and had come to the wilderness of Sinai, they encamped in the wilderness; and there Yisra'el encamped before the mountain. Moshe went up to God, and the LORD called to him out of the mountain, saying, "This is what you shall tell the house of Ya`akov, and tell the children of Yisra'el: 'You have seen what I did to the Egyptians, and how I bore you on eagles' wings, and brought you to Myself. Now therefore, if you will indeed obey My voice, and keep My covenant, then you shall be My own possession from among all peoples; for all the earth is Mine; and you shall be to Me a kingdom of Kohanim, and a holy nation.' These are the words which you shall speak to the children of Yisra'el." Moshe came and called for the elders of the people, and set before them all these words which the LORD commanded him. All the people answered together, and said, "All that the LORD has spoken we will do." Moshe reported the words of the people to the LORD.

Haftarah

Isaiah 6:9-12

He said, "Go, and tell this people, 'You hear indeed, but don't understand; and you see indeed, but don't perceive.' Make the heart of this people fat. Make their ears heavy, and shut their eyes; lest they see with their eyes, and hear with their ears, and understand with their heart, and turn again, and be healed." Then I said, "Lord, how long?" He answered, "Until cities are waste without inhabitant, and houses without man, and the land becomes utterly waste, And the LORD has removed men far away, and the forsaken places are many in the midst of the land.

Brit Chadasha

1 Timothy 3:1-13

Parashat Yitro — Day 3

This is a faithful saying: if a man seeks the office of an overseer, he desires a good work. The overseer therefore must be without reproach, the husband of one wife, temperate, sensible, modest, hospitable, good at teaching; not a drinker, not violent, not greedy for money, but gentle, not quarrelsome, not covetous; one who rules his own house well, having children in subjection with all reverence; (but if a man doesn't know how to rule his own house, how will he take care of the assembly of God?) not a new convert, lest being puffed up he fall into the same condemnation as the devil. Moreover he must have good testimony from those who are outside, to avoid falling into reproach and the snare of the devil. Servants, in the same way, must be reverent, not double-tongued, not addicted to much wine, not greedy for money; holding the mystery of the faith in a pure conscience. Let them also first be tested; then let them serve if they are blameless. Their wives in the same way must be reverent, not slanderers, temperate, faithful in all things. Let servants be husbands of one wife, ruling their children and their own houses well. For those who have served well gain for themselves a good standing, and great boldness in the faith which is in Messiah Yeshua.

1 Peter 2:9-10

But you are a chosen race, a royal priesthood, a holy nation, a people for God's own possession, that you may proclaim the excellence of Him who called you out of darkness into His marvelous light: who in time past were no people, but now are God's people, who had not obtained mercy, but now have obtained mercy.

Acts 6:1-7

Now in those days, when the number of the talmidim was multiplying, a complaint arose from the Hellenists against the Hebrews, because their widows were neglected in the daily service. The twelve summoned the multitude of the talmidim and said, "It is not appropriate for us to forsake the word of God and serve tables. Therefore select from among you, brothers, seven men of good report, full of the Holy Spirit and of wisdom, whom we may appoint over this business. But we will continue steadfastly in prayer and in the ministry of the word." These words pleased the whole multitude. They chose Stephen, a man full of faith and of the Holy Spirit, Philip, Prochorus, Nicanor, Timon, Parmenas, and Nicolaus, a proselyte of Antioch; whom they set before the emissaries. When they had prayed, they laid their hands on them. The word of God increased and the number of the talmidim multiplied in Yerushalayim exceedingly. A great company of the Kohanim were obedient to the faith.

Parashat: Yitro - "Jethro"

Daily Portion: Wednesday

Parashat Yitro Day 4

Exodus 19:9-19

The LORD said to Moshe, "Behold, I come to you in a thick cloud, that the people may hear when I speak with you, and may also believe you forever." Moshe told the words of the people to the LORD.

The LORD said to Moshe, "Go to the people, and sanctify them today and tomorrow, and let them wash their garments, and be ready against the third day; for on the third day the LORD will come down in the sight of all the people on Mount Sinai. You shall set bounds to the people round about, saying, 'Be careful that you don't go up onto the mountain, or touch its border.

Whoever touches the mountain shall be surely put to death. No hand shall touch him, but he shall surely be stoned or shot through; whether it is animal or man, he shall not live.' When the shofar sounds long, they shall come up to the mountain."

Moshe went down from the mountain to the people, and sanctified the people; and they washed their clothes. He said to the people, "Be ready by the third day. Don't have sexual relations with a woman."

It happened on the third day, when it was morning, that there were thunders and lightnings, and a thick cloud on the mountain, and the sound of an exceedingly loud shofar; and all the people who were in the camp trembled.

Moshe led the people out of the camp to meet God; and they stood at the lower part of the mountain. Mount Sinai, the whole of it, smoked, because the LORD descended on it in fire; and its smoke ascended like the smoke of a furnace, and the whole mountain quaked greatly.

When the sound of the shofar grew louder and louder, Moshe spoke, and God answered him by a voice.

Haftarah

Isaiah 6:13-7:2

If there are yet a tenth in it, it also shall in turn be eaten up: as a terebinth, and as an oak, whose stock remains, when they are felled; so the holy seed is its stock."

It happened in the days of Achaz the son of Yotam, the son of 'Uzziyah, king of Yehudah, that Retzin the king of Syria, and Pekach the son of Remalyahu, king of Yisra'el, went up to Yerushalayim to war against it, but could not prevail against it.

It was told the house of David, saying, "Syria is allied with Efrayim." His heart trembled, and the heart of his people, as the trees of the forest tremble with the wind.

Parashat Yitro — Day 4

Brit Chadasha

Hebrews 12:18-29

For you have not come to a mountain that might be touched, and that burned with fire, and to blackness, darkness, storm, the sound of a shofar, and the voice of words; which those who heard it begged that not one more word should be spoken to them, for they could not stand that which was commanded, "If even an animal touches the mountain, it shall be stoned;" and so fearful was the appearance, that Moshe said, "I am terrified and trembling."

But you have come to Mount Tziyon, and to the city of the living God, the heavenly Yerushalayim, and to innumerable multitudes of angels, to the general assembly and assembly of the firstborn who are enrolled in heaven, to God the Judge of all, to the spirits of just men made perfect, to Yeshua, the mediator of a new covenant, and to the blood of sprinkling that speaks better than that of Hevel.

See that you don't refuse Him who speaks. For if they didn't escape when they refused Him who warned on the Earth, how much more will we not escape who turn away from Him who warns from heaven, whose voice shook the earth then, but now He has promised, saying, "Yet once more I will shake not only the earth, but also the heavens."

This phrase, "Yet once more," signifies the removing of those things that are shaken, as of things that have been made, that those things which are not shaken may remain.

Therefore, receiving a Kingdom that can't be shaken, let us have grace, through which we serve God acceptably, with reverence and awe, for our God is a consuming fire.

Parashat: Yitro - "Jethro"

Daily Portion: Thursday

Exodus 19:20-7

The LORD came down on Mount Sinai, to the top of the mountain. The LORD called Moshe to the top of the mountain, and Moshe went up. The LORD said to Moshe, "Go down, charge the people, lest they break through to the LORD to gaze, and many of them perish. Let the Kohanim also, who come near to the LORD, sanctify themselves, lest the LORD break forth on them." Moshe said to the LORD, "The people can't come up to Mount Sinai, for you charged us, saying, 'Set bounds around the mountain, and sanctify it.'" The LORD said to him, "Go down and you shall bring Aharon up with you, but don't let the Kohanim and the people break through to come up to the LORD, lest He break forth on them." So Moshe went down to the people, and told them.

God spoke all these words, saying,

"I am the LORD your God, who brought you out of the land of Egypt, out of the house of bondage. You shall have no other gods before Me.

"You shall not make for yourselves an idol, nor any image of anything that is in the heavens above, or that is in the earth beneath, or that is in the water under the earth: you shall not bow yourself down to them, nor serve them, for I, the LORD your God, am a jealous God, visiting the iniquity of the fathers on the children, on the third and on the fourth generation of those who hate Me, and showing loving kindness to thousands of those who love Me and keep My mitzvot.

"You shall not take the name of the LORD your God in vain, for the LORD will not hold him guiltless who takes His name in vain.

Haftarah

Isaiah 7:3-6

Then the LORD said to Yeshaiyahu, "Go out now to meet Achaz, you, and She'ar-Yashuv your son, at the end of the conduit of the upper pool, on the highway of the fuller's field.

Tell him, 'Be careful, and keep calm. Don't be afraid, neither let your heart be faint because of these two tails of smoking firebrands, for the fierce anger of Retzin and Syria, and of the son of Remalyahu.

Because Syria, Efrayim, and the son of Remalyahu, have plotted evil against you, saying, "Let's go up against Yehudah, and tear it apart, and let's divide it among ourselves, and set up a king in the midst of it, even the son of Tav'el."

Parashat Yitro

Day 5

Brit Chadasha

Romans 2:17-29

Indeed you bear the name of a Jew, and rest on the law, and glory in God, and know his will, and approve the things that are excellent, being instructed out of the Torah, and are confident that you yourself are a guide of the blind, a light to those who are in darkness, a corrector of the foolish, a teacher of babies, having in the law the form of knowledge and of the truth.

You therefore who teach another, don't you teach yourself?

You who preach that a man shouldn't steal, do you steal?

You who say a man shouldn't commit adultery, do you commit adultery?

You who abhor idols, do you rob temples?

You who glory in the law, through your disobedience of the law do you dishonor God?

For "the name of God is blasphemed among the Gentiles because of you," just as it is written.

For circumcision indeed profits, if you are a doer of the law, but if you are a transgressor of the law, your circumcision has become uncircumcision.

If therefore the uncircumcised keep the ordinances of the law, won't his uncircumcision be accounted as circumcision?

Won't the uncircumcision which is by nature, if it fulfills the law, judge you, who with the letter and circumcision are a transgressor of the law?

For he is not a Jew who is one outwardly, neither is that circumcision which is outward in the flesh; but he is a Jew who is one inwardly, and circumcision is that of the heart, in the spirit not in the letter; whose praise is not from men, but from God.

Parashat: Yitro - "Jethro"

Daily Portion: Friday

Exodus 20:8-(23)26

Parashat Yitro — Day 6

"Remember the day of Shabbat, to keep it holy. You shall labor six days, and do all your work, but the seventh day is a Shabbat to the LORD your God. You shall not do any work in it, you, nor your son, nor your daughter, your male servant, nor your female servant, nor your livestock, nor your stranger who is within your gates; for in six days the LORD made heaven and earth, the sea, and all that is in them, and rested the seventh day; therefore the LORD blessed the day of Shabbat, and made it holy.

"Honor your father and your mother, that your days may be long in the land which the LORD your God gives you.

"You shall not murder.

"You shall not commit adultery.

"You shall not steal.

"You shall not give false testimony against your neighbor.

"You shall not covet your neighbor's house. You shall not covet your neighbor's wife, nor his male servant, nor his female servant, nor his ox, nor his donkey, nor anything that is your neighbor's."

All the people perceived the thunderings, the lightnings, the sound of the shofar, and the mountain smoking.

When the people saw it, they trembled, and stayed at a distance. They said to Moshe, "Speak with us yourself, and we will listen; but don't let God speak with us, lest we die."

Moshe said to the people, "Don't be afraid, for God has come to test you, and that His fear may be before you, that you won't sin."

The people stayed at a distance, and Moshe drew near to the thick darkness where God was.

The LORD said to Moshe, "This is what you shall tell the children of Yisra'el: 'You yourselves have seen that I have talked with you from heaven. You shall most certainly not make alongside of Me gods of silver, or gods of gold for yourselves.

Haftarah

Isaiah 9:5-6(6-7)

Parashat Yitro
Day 6

For to us a Child is born. To us a Son is given; and the government will be on His shoulders. His name will be called Wonderful, Counselor, Mighty God, Everlasting Father, Prince of Shalom. Of the increase of His government and of shalom there shall be no end, on the throne of David, and on His kingdom, to establish it, and to uphold it with justice and with righteousness from that time on, even forever. The zeal of the LORD of Armies will perform this.

Brit Chadasha

James 2:8-13

However, if you fulfill the royal Torah, according to the Scripture, "You shall love your neighbor as yourself," you do well. But if you show partiality, you commit sin, being convicted by the Torah as transgressors. For whoever keeps the whole Torah, and yet stumbles in one point, he has become guilty of all. For He who said, "Do not commit adultery," also said, "Do not commit murder." Now if you do not commit adultery, but murder, you have become a transgressor of the law. So speak, and so do, as men who are to be judged by a law of freedom. For judgment is without mercy to him who has shown no mercy. Mercy triumphs over judgment.

Romans 7:7-12

What shall we say then? Is the law sin? May it never be! However, I wouldn't have known sin, except through the law. For I wouldn't have known coveting, unless the law had said, "You shall not covet." But sin, finding occasion through the mitzvah, produced in me all kinds of coveting. For apart from the law, sin is dead. I was alive apart from the law once, but when the mitzvah came, sin revived, and I died. The mitzvah, which was for life, this I found to be for death; for sin, finding occasion through the mitzvah, deceived me, and through it killed me. Therefore the law indeed is holy, and the mitzvah holy, and righteous, and good.

Parashat Yitro
Day 7

Special Shabbat Readings

Daily Portion: Shabbat

Isaiah 56:1-7

Thus says the LORD, Keep you justice, and do righteousness; for My yeshu`ah is near to come, and My righteousness to be revealed.

Blessed is the man who does this, and the son of man who holds it fast; who keeps the Shabbat from profaning it, and keeps his hand from doing any evil.

Neither let the foreigner, who has joined himself to the LORD, speak, saying, the LORD will surely separate me from His people; neither let the eunuch say, Behold, I am a dry tree.

For thus says the LORD of the eunuchs who keep My Shabbatot, and choose the things that please Me, and hold fast my covenant:

To them will I give in My house and within My walls a memorial and a name better than of sons and of daughters; I will give them an everlasting name, that shall not be cut off.

Also the foreigners who join themselves to the LORD, to minister to Him, and to love the name of the LORD, to be His servants, everyone who keeps the Shabbat from profaning it, and holds fast My covenant; even them will I bring to My holy mountain, and make them joyful in My house of prayer: their burnt offerings and their sacrifices shall be accepted on My altar; for My house shall be called a house of prayer for all peoples.

Isaiah 58:13-14

If you turn away your foot from the Shabbat, from doing your pleasure on My holy day; and call the Shabbat a delight, [and] the holy of the LORD honorable; and shall honor it, not doing your own ways, nor finding your own pleasure, nor speaking [your own] words: then shall you delight yourself in the LORD; and I will make you to ride on the high places of the earth; and I will feed you with the heritage of Ya`akov your father: for the mouth of the LORD has spoken it.

Psalm 92

<<A Psalm. A song for the day of Shabbat.>>

Parashat Yitro — Day 7

It is a good thing to give thanks to the LORD, to sing praises to Your name, Elyon; to proclaim Your loving kindness in the morning, and Your faithfulness every night, with the ten-stringed lute, with the harp, and with the melody of the lyre.

For You, LORD, have made me glad through your work. I will triumph in the works of Your hands.

How great are Your works, LORD! Your thoughts are very deep.

A senseless man doesn't know, neither does a fool understand this: though the wicked spring up as the grass, and all the evil-doers flourish, they will be destroyed forever.

But You, LORD, are on high forevermore.

For, behold, Your enemies, LORD, for, behold, Your enemies shall perish. All the evil-doers will be scattered.

But You have exalted my horn like that of the wild ox. I am anointed with fresh oil.

My eye has also seen my enemies. My ears have heard of the wicked enemies who rise up against me.

The righteous shall flourish like the palm tree. He will grow like a cedar in Levanon.

They are planted in the LORD's house. They will flourish in our God's courts.

They will still bring forth fruit in old age. They will be full of sap and green, to show that the LORD is upright. He is my rock, and there is no unrighteousness in Him.

Hebrews 4:8-11

For if Yehoshua had given them rest, He would not have spoken afterward of another day. There remains therefore a Shabbat rest for the people of God. For he who has entered into His rest has himself also rested from his works, as God did from His. Let us therefore give diligence to enter into that rest, lest anyone fall after the same example of disobedience.

Parashat: Mishpatim - "Ordinances"

Daily Portion: Sunday

Exodus 21:1-19

"Now these are the ordinances which you shall set before them. "If you buy a Hebrew servant, he shall serve six years and in the seventh he shall go out free without paying anything. If he comes in by himself, he shall go out by himself.

If he is married, then his wife shall go out with him. If his master gives him a wife and she bears him sons or daughters, the wife and her children shall be her master's, and he shall go out by himself.

But if the servant shall plainly say, 'I love my master, my wife, and my children. I will not go out free;' then his master shall bring him to God, and shall bring him to the door or to the doorpost, and his master shall bore his ear through with an awl, and he shall serve him for ever.

"If a man sells his daughter to be a female servant, she shall not go out as the male servants do. If she doesn't please her master, who has married her to himself, then he shall let her be redeemed. He shall have no right to sell her to a foreign people, seeing he has dealt deceitfully with her.

If he marries her to his son, he shall deal with her after the manner of daughters. If he takes another wife to himself, he shall not diminish her food, her clothing, and her marital rights. If he doesn't do these three things for her, she may go free without paying any money.

"One who strikes a man so that he dies shall surely be put to death, but not if it is unintentional, but God allows it to happen: then I will appoint you a place where he shall flee. If a man schemes and comes presumptuously on his neighbor to kill him, you shall take him from my altar, that he may die.

"Anyone who attacks his father or his mother shall be surely put to death. "Anyone who kidnaps someone and sells him, or if he is found in his hand, he shall surely be put to death. "Anyone who curses his father or his mother shall surely be put to death.

"If men quarrel and one strikes the other with a stone, or with his fist, and he doesn't die, but is confined to bed; if he rises again and walks around with his staff, then he who struck him shall be cleared: only he shall pay for the loss of his time, and shall provide for his healing until he is thoroughly healed.

Haftarah

Jeremiah 34:8-9

The word that came to Yirmeyahu from the LORD, after that the king Tzidkiyahu had made a covenant with all the people who were at Yerushalayim, to proclaim liberty to them; that every man should let his male servant, and every man his female servant, who is a Hebrew or a Hebrewess, go free; that none should make bondservants of them, [to wit], of a Jew his brother.

Parashat Mishpatim — Day 1

Brit Chadasha

Hebrews 10:28-39

A man who disregards the Torah of Moshe dies without compassion on the word of two or three witnesses. How much worse punishment, do you think, will he be judged worthy of, who has trodden under foot the Son of God, and has counted the blood of the covenant with which he was sanctified an unholy thing, and has insulted the Spirit of grace?

For we know Him who said, "Vengeance belongs to Me," says the Lord, "I will repay." Again, "The Lord will judge His people." It is a fearful thing to fall into the hands of the living God.

But remember the former days, in which, after you were enlightened, you endured a great struggle with sufferings; partly, being exposed to both reproaches and oppressions; and partly, becoming partakers with those who were treated so.

For you both had compassion on me in my chains, and joyfully accepted the plundering of your possessions, knowing that you have for yourselves a better possession and an enduring one in the heavens. Therefore don't throw away your boldness, which has a great reward.

For you need endurance so that, having done the will of God, you may receive the promise. "In a very little while, He who comes will come, and will not wait.

But the righteous will live by faith. If he shrinks back, my soul has no pleasure in him." But we are not of those who shrink back to destruction, but of those who have faith to the saving of the soul.

Parashat: Mishpatim - "Ordinances"

Daily Portion: Monday

Exodus 21:20-36

"If a man strikes his servant or his maid with a rod, and he dies under his hand, he shall surely be punished. Notwithstanding, if he gets up after a day or two, he shall not be punished, for he is his property.

"If men fight and hurt a pregnant woman so that she gives birth prematurely, and yet no harm follows, he shall be surely fined as much as the woman's husband demands and the judges allow.

But if any harm follows, then you must take life for life, eye for eye, tooth for tooth, hand for hand, foot for foot, burning for burning, wound for wound, and bruise for bruise.

"If a man strikes his servant's eye, or his maid's eye, and destroys it, he shall let him go free for his eye's sake. If he strikes out his male servant's tooth, or his female servant's tooth, he shall let him go free for his tooth's sake.

"If a bull gores a man or a woman to death, the bull shall surely be stoned, and its flesh shall not be eaten; but the owner of the bull shall not be held responsible.

But if the bull had a habit of goring in the past, and it has been testified to its owner, and he has not kept it in, but it has killed a man or a woman, the bull shall be stoned, and its owner shall also be put to death.

If a ransom is laid on him, then he shall give for the redemption of his life whatever is laid on him. Whether it has gored a son or has gored a daughter, according to this judgment it shall be done to him.

If the bull gores a male servant or a female servant, thirty shekels of silver shall be given to their master, and the ox shall be stoned.

"If a man opens a pit, or if a man digs a pit and doesn't cover it, and a bull or a donkey falls into it, the owner of the pit shall make it good. He shall give money to its owner, and the dead animal shall be his.

"If one man's bull injures another's, so that it dies, then they shall sell the live bull, and divide its price; and they shall also divide the dead animal.

Or if it is known that the bull was in the habit of goring in the past, and its owner has not kept it in, he shall surely pay bull for bull, and the dead animal shall be his own.

Haftarah

Jeremiah 34:10-11

All the princes and all the people obeyed, who had entered into the covenant, that everyone should let his male servant, and everyone his female servant, go free, that none should make bondservants of them any more; they obeyed, and let them go: but afterwards they turned, and caused the servants and the handmaids, whom they had let go free, to return, and brought them into subjection for servants and for handmaids.

Parashat Mishpatim — Day 2

Brit Chadasha

Matthew 5:38-42

"You have heard that it was said, 'An eye for an eye, and a tooth for a tooth.' But I tell you, don't resist him who is evil; but whoever strikes you on your right cheek, turn to him the other also. If anyone sues you to take away your coat, let him have your cloak also. Whoever compels you to go one mile, go with him two. Give to him who asks you, and don't turn away him who desires to borrow from you.

Romans 2:1-11

Therefore you are without excuse, O man, whoever you are who judge. For in that which you judge another, you condemn yourself. For you who judge practice the same things. We know that the judgment of God is according to truth against those who practice such things. Do you think this, O man who judges those who practice such things, and do the same, that you will escape the judgment of God? Or do you despise the riches of His goodness, forbearance, and patience, not knowing that the goodness of God leads you to repentance? But according to your hardness and unrepentant heart you are treasuring up for yourself wrath in the day of wrath, revelation, and of the righteous judgment of God; who "will pay back to everyone according to their works:" to those who by patience in well-doing seek for glory and honor and incorruptibility, eternal life; but to those who are self-seeking, and don't obey the truth, but obey unrighteousness, will be wrath and indignation, oppression and anguish, on every soul of man who works evil, on the Jew first, and also on the Greek. But glory and honor and shalom to every man who works good, to the Jew first, and also to the Greek. For there is no partiality with God.

Parashat Mishpatim
Day 3

Parashat: Mishpatim - "Ordinances"

Daily Portion: Tuesday

Exodus 22:1-17

"If a man steals an ox or a sheep, and kills it, or sells it; he shall pay five oxen for an ox, and four sheep for a sheep. If the thief is found breaking in, and is struck so that he dies, there shall be no guilt of bloodshed for him. If the sun has risen on him, there shall be guilt of bloodshed for him; he shall make restitution. If he has nothing, then he shall be sold for his theft. If the stolen property is found in his hand alive, whether it is ox, donkey, or sheep, he shall pay double. "If a man causes a field or vineyard to be eaten, and lets his animal loose, and it grazes in another man's field, he shall make restitution from the best of his own field, and from the best of his own vineyard. "If fire breaks out, and catches in thorns so that the shocks of grain, or the standing grain, or the field are consumed; he who kindled the fire shall surely make restitution. "If a man delivers to his neighbor money or stuff to keep, and it is stolen out of the man's house; if the thief is found, he shall pay double. If the thief isn't found, then the master of the house shall come near to God, to find out if he hasn't put his hand to his neighbor's goods.

For every matter of trespass, whether it be for ox, for donkey, for sheep, for clothing, or for any kind of lost thing, about which one says, 'This is mine,' the cause of both parties shall come before God. He whom God condemns shall pay double to his neighbor. "If a man delivers to his neighbor a donkey, an ox, a sheep, or any animal to keep, and it dies or is injured, or driven away, no man seeing it; the oath of the LORD shall be between them both, whether he hasn't put his hand to his neighbor's goods; and the owner of it shall accept it, and he shall not make restitution. But if it is stolen from him, he shall make restitution to the owner of it. If it is torn in pieces, let him bring it for evidence. He shall not make good that which was torn. "If a man borrows anything of his neighbor's, and it is injured, or dies, the owner of it not being with it, he shall surely make restitution. If the owner of it is with it, he shall not make it good. If it is a leased thing, it came for its lease. "If a man entices a virgin who isn't pledged to be married, and lies with her, he shall surely pay a dowry for her to be his wife. If her father utterly refuses to give her to him, he shall pay money according to the dowry of virgins.

Haftarah

Jeremiah 34:12-14

Therefore the word of the LORD came to Yirmeyahu from the LORD, saying, Thus says the LORD, the God of Yisra'el: I made a covenant with your fathers in the day that I brought them forth out of the land of Egypt, out of the house of bondage, saying, At the end of seven years you shall let go every man his brother who is a Hebrew, who has been sold to you, and has served you six years, you shall let him go free from you: but your fathers didn't listen to Me, neither inclined their ear.

Parashat Mishpatim
Day 3

Brit Chadasha

Romans 2:12-29

For as many as have sinned without law will also perish without the law. As many as have sinned under the law will be judged by the law. For it isn't the hearers of the law who are righteous before God, but the doers of the law will be justified (for when Gentiles who don't have the law do by nature the things of the law, these, not having the law, are a law to themselves, in that they show the work of the law written in their hearts, their conscience testifying with them, and their thoughts among themselves accusing or else excusing them) in the day when God will judge the secrets of men, according to my Good News, by Yeshua the Messiah. Indeed you bear the name of a Jew, and rest on the law, and glory in God, and know his will, and approve the things that are excellent, being instructed out of the Torah, and are confident that you yourself are a guide of the blind, a light to those who are in darkness, a corrector of the foolish, a teacher of babies, having in the law the form of knowledge and of the truth.

You therefore who teach another, don't you teach yourself? You who preach that a man shouldn't steal, do you steal? You who say a man shouldn't commit adultery, do you commit adultery? You who abhor idols, do you rob temples? You who glory in the law, through your disobedience of the law do you dishonor God? For "the name of God is blasphemed among the Gentiles because of you," Just as it is written. For circumcision indeed profits, if you are a doer of the law, but if you are a transgressor of the law, your circumcision has become uncircumcision. If therefore the uncircumcised keep the ordinances of the law, won't his uncircumcision be accounted as circumcision? Won't the uncircumcision which is by nature, if it fulfills the law, judge you, who with the letter and circumcision are a transgressor of the law? For he is not a Jew who is one outwardly, neither is that circumcision which is outward in the flesh; but he is a Jew who is one inwardly, and circumcision is that of the heart, in the spirit not in the letter; whose praise is not from men, but from God.

Parashat: Mishpatim - "Ordinances"

Daily Portion: Wednesday

Exodus 22:18-23:9

"You shall not allow a sorceress to live. "Whoever has sex with an animal shall surely be put to death. "He who sacrifices to any god, except to the LORD only, shall be utterly destroyed. "You shall not wrong an alien, neither shall you oppress him, for you were aliens in the land of Egypt. "You shall not take advantage of any widow or fatherless child. If you take advantage of them at all, and they cry at all to me, I will surely hear their cry; and my wrath will grow hot, and I will kill you with the sword; and your wives shall be widows, and your children fatherless. "If you lend money to any of my people with you who is poor, you shall not be to him as a creditor; neither shall you charge him interest. If you take your neighbor's garment as collateral, you shall restore it to him before the sun goes down, for that is his only covering, it is his garment for his skin. What would he sleep in? It will happen, when he cries to me, that I will hear, for I am gracious. "You shall not blaspheme God, nor curse a ruler of your people. "You shall not delay to offer from your harvest and from the outflow of your presses. "You shall give the firstborn of your sons to me. You shall do likewise with your oxen and with your sheep. Seven days it shall be with its mother, then on the eighth day you shall give it me. "You shall be holy men to me, therefore you shall not eat any flesh that is torn by animals in the field. You shall cast it to the dogs. "You shall not spread a false report. Don't join your hand with the wicked to be a malicious witness. You shall not follow a crowd to do evil; neither shall you testify in court to side with a multitude to pervert justice; neither shall you favor a poor man in his cause. "If you meet your enemy's ox or his donkey going astray, you shall surely bring it back to him again. If you see the donkey of him who hates you fallen down under his burden, don't leave him, you shall surely help him with it. "You shall not deny justice to your poor people in their lawsuits. "Keep far from a false charge, and don't kill the innocent and righteous: for I will not justify the wicked. "You shall take no bribe, for a bribe blinds those who have sight and perverts the words of the righteous. "You shall not oppress an alien, for you know the heart of an alien, seeing you were aliens in the land of Egypt.

Haftarah

Jeremiah 34:15-17

You were now turned, and had done that which is right in My eyes, in proclaiming liberty every man to his neighbor; and you had made a covenant before Me in the house which is called by My name:but you turned and profaned My name, and caused every man his servant, and every man his handmaid, whom you had let go free at their pleasure, to return; and you brought them into subjection, to be to you for servants and for handmaids. Therefore thus says the LORD: you have not listened to Me, to proclaim liberty, every man to his brother, and every man to his neighbor: behold, I proclaim to you a liberty, says the LORD, to the sword, to the pestilence, and to the famine; and I will make you to be tossed back and forth among all the kingdoms of the earth.

Parashat Mishpatim Day 4

Brit Chadasha

Acts 23:1-16

Sha'ul, looking steadfastly at the council, said, "Brothers, I have lived before God in all good conscience until this day." The Kohen Gadol, Chananyah, commanded those who stood by him to strike him on the mouth. Then Sha'ul said to him, "God will strike you, you whitewashed wall! Do you sit to judge me according to the Torah, and command me to be struck contrary to the Torah?" Those who stood by said, "Do you malign God's Kohen Gadol?" Sha'ul said, "I didn't know, brothers, that he was Kohen Gadol. For it is written, 'You shall not speak evil of a ruler of your people.'" But when Sha'ul perceived that the one part were Tzedukim and the other Perushim, he cried out in the council, "Men and brothers, I am a Parush, a son of Perushim. Concerning the hope and resurrection of the dead I am being judged!" When he had said this, an argument arose between the Perushim and Tzedukim, and the assembly was divided. For the Tzedukim say that there is no resurrection, nor angel, nor spirit; but the Perushim confess all of these. A great clamor arose, and some of the scribes of the Perushim part stood up, and contended, saying, "We find no evil in this man. But if a spirit or angel has spoken to him, let's not fight against God!" When a great argument arose, the commanding officer, fearing that Sha'ul would be torn in pieces by them, commanded the soldiers to go down and take him by force from among them, and bring him into the barracks. The following night, the Lord stood by him, and said, "Cheer up, Sha'ul, for as you have testified about Me at Yerushalayim, so you must testify also at Rome." When it was day, some of the Judeans banded together, and bound themselves under a curse, saying that they would neither eat nor drink until they had killed Sha'ul. There were more than forty people who had made this conspiracy. They came to the chief Kohanim and the elders, and said, "We have bound ourselves under a great curse, to taste nothing until we have killed Sha'ul. Now therefore, you with the council inform the commanding officer that he should bring him down to you tomorrow, as though you were going to judge his case more exactly. We are ready to kill him before he comes near." But Sha'ul's sister's son heard of their lying in wait, and he came and entered into the barracks and told Sha'ul.

Parashat: Mishpatim - "Ordinances"

Daily Portion: Thursday

Exodus 23:10-26

"For six years you shall sow your land, and shall gather in its increase, but the seventh year you shall let it rest and lie fallow, that the poor of your people may eat; and what they leave the animal of the field shall eat. In like manner you shall deal with your vineyard and with your olive grove. "Six days you shall do your work, and on the seventh day you shall rest, that your ox and your donkey may have rest, and the son of your handmaid, and the alien may be refreshed. "Be careful to do all things that I have said to you; and don't invoke the name of other gods, neither let them be heard out of your mouth. "You shall observe a feast to Me three times a year. You shall observe the feast of matzah. Seven days you shall eat matzah, as I commanded you, at the time appointed in the month Aviv (for in it you came out from Egypt), and no one shall appear before Me empty.

And the Chag-HaKatzir, the first fruits of your labors, which you sow in the field: and the Chag-HaKatzir, at the end of the year, when you gather in your labors out of the field. Three times in the year all your males shall appear before the Lord GOD. "You shall not offer the blood of My sacrifice with leavened bread, neither shall the fat of My feast remain all night until the morning. The first of the first fruits of your ground you shall bring into the house of the LORD your God. "You shall not boil a kid in its mother's milk. "Behold, I send an Angel before you, to keep you by the way, and to bring you into the place which I have prepared. Pay attention to Him, and listen to His voice. Don't provoke Him, for He will not pardon your disobedience, for My name is in Him. But if you indeed listen to His voice, and do all that I speak, then I will be an enemy to your enemies, and an adversary to your adversaries. For My Angel shall go before you, and bring you in to the Amori, the Chittite, the Perizzi, the Kena'ani, the Chivvi, and the Yevusi; and I will cut them off. You shall not bow down to their gods, nor serve them, nor follow their practices, but you shall utterly overthrow them and demolish their pillars. You shall serve the LORD your God, and He will bless your bread and your water, and I will take sickness away from your midst. No one will miscarry or be barren in your land. I will fulfill the number of your days.

Haftarah

Jeremiah 34:18-20

I will give the men who have transgressed My covenant, who have not performed the words of the covenant which they made before Me, when they cut the calf in two and passed between the parts of it; the princes of Yehudah, and the princes of Yerushalayim, the eunuchs, and the Kohanim, and all the people of the land, who passed between the parts of the calf; I will even give them into the hand of their enemies, and into the hand of those who seek their life; and their dead bodies shall be for food to the birds of the sky, and to the animals of the earth.

Parashat Mishpatim

Day 5

Brit Chadasha

Matthew 12:1-18

At that time, Yeshua went on the day of Shabbat through the grain fields. His talmidim were hungry and began to pluck heads of grain and to eat. But the Perushim, when they saw it, said to him, "Behold, Your talmidim do what is not lawful to do on the Shabbat." But He said to them, "Haven't you read what David did, when he was hungry, and those who were with him; how he entered into the house of God, and ate the show bread, which was not lawful for him to eat, neither for those who were with him, but only for the Kohanim? Or have you not read in the Torah, that on the day of Shabbat, the Kohanim in the temple profane the Shabbat, and are guiltless? But I tell you that one greater than the temple is here. But if you had known what this means, 'I desire mercy, and not sacrifice,' you would not have condemned the guiltless. For the Son of Man is Lord of the Shabbat."

He departed there, and went into their synagogue. And behold there was a man with a withered hand. They asked Him, "Is it lawful to heal on the day of Shabbat?" that they might accuse Him. He said to them, "What man is there among you, who has one sheep, and if this one falls into a pit on the day of Shabbat, won't he grab on to it, and lift it out? Of how much more value then is a man than a sheep! Therefore it is lawful to do good on the day of Shabbat." Then He told the man, "Stretch out your hand." He stretched it out; and it was restored whole, just like the other. But the Perushim went out, and conspired against Him, how they might destroy Him. Yeshua, perceiving that, withdrew from there. Great multitudes followed Him; and He healed them all, and charged them that they should not make Him known: that it might be fulfilled which was spoken through Yeshaiyahu the prophet, saying, "Behold, My servant whom I have chosen; My beloved in whom My soul is well pleased: I will put My Spirit on him. He will proclaim justice to the nations.

Parashat: Mishpatim – "Ordinances"

Daily Portion: Friday

Exodus 23:27-24:11

I will send My terror before you, and will confuse all the people to whom you come, and I will make all your enemies turn their backs to you. I will send the hornet before you, which will drive out the Chivvi, the Kena'ani, and the Chittite, from before you. I will not drive them out from before you in one year, lest the land become desolate, and the animals of the field multiply against you.

Little by little I will drive them out from before you, until you have increased and inherit the land. I will set your border from the Sea of Suf even to the sea of the Pelishtim, and from the wilderness to the River; for I will deliver the inhabitants of the land into your hand, and you shall drive them out before you. You shall make no covenant with them, nor with their gods. They shall not dwell in your land, lest they make you sin against Me, for if you serve their gods, it will surely be a snare to you."

He said to Moshe, "Come up to the LORD, you, and Aharon, Nadav, and Avihu, and seventy of the elders of Yisra'el; and worship from a distance. Moshe alone shall come near to the LORD, but they shall not come near, neither shall the people go up with him." Moshe came and told the people all the words of the LORD, and all the ordinances; and all the people answered with one voice, and said, "All the words which the LORD has spoken will we do."

Moshe wrote all the words of the LORD, and rose up early in the morning, and built an altar under the mountain, and twelve pillars for the twelve tribes of Yisra'el. He sent young men of the children of Yisra'el, who offered burnt offerings and sacrificed shalom offerings of oxen to the LORD. Moshe took half of the blood and put it in basins, and half of the blood he sprinkled on the altar. He took the book of the covenant and read it in the hearing of the people, and they said, "All that the LORD has spoken will we do, and be obedient."

Moshe took the blood, and sprinkled it on the people, and said, "Look, this is the blood of the covenant, which the LORD has made with you concerning all these words." Then Moshe, Aharon, Nadav, Avihu, and seventy of the elders of Yisra'el went up. They saw the God of Yisra'el. Under his feet was like a paved work of sappir stone, like the skies for clearness. He didn't lay his hand on the nobles of the children of Yisra'el. They saw God, and ate and drank.

Haftarah

Jeremiah 34:21-22

Tzidkiyahu king of Yehudah and his princes will I give into the hand of their enemies, and into the hand of those who seek their life, and into the hand of the king of Bavel's army, who have gone away from you.

Behold, I will command, says the LORD, and cause them to return to this city; and they shall fight against it, and take it, and burn it with fire: and I will make the cities of Yehudah a desolation, without inhabitant.

Parashat Mishpatim — Day 6

Brit Chadasha

Hebrews 9:15-22

For this reason He is the mediator of a new covenant, since a death has occurred for the redemption of the transgressions that were under the first covenant, that those who have been called may receive the promise of the eternal inheritance.

For where a last will and testament is, there must of necessity be the death of him who made it.

For a will is in force where there has been death, for it is never in force while he who made it lives.

Therefore even the first covenant has not been dedicated without blood.

For when every mitzvah had been spoken by Moshe to all the people according to the Torah, he took the blood of the calves and the goats, with water and scarlet wool and hyssop, and sprinkled both the book itself and all the people, saying, "This is the blood of the covenant which God has commanded you."

Moreover he sprinkled the tabernacle and all the vessels of the ministry in like manner with the blood.

According to the Torah, nearly everything is cleansed with blood, and apart from shedding of blood there is no remission.

Parashat: Mishpatim - "Ordinances"

Daily Portion: Shabbat

Exodus 24:12-18

The LORD said to Moshe, "Come up to Me on the mountain, and stay here, and I will give you the tables of stone with the law and the commands that I have written, that you may teach them."

Moshe rose up with Yehoshua, his servant, and Moshe went up onto God's Mountain. He said to the elders, "Wait here for us, until we come again to you. Behold, Aharon and Chur are with you.

Whoever is involved in a dispute can go to them." Moshe went up on the mountain, and the cloud covered the mountain. The glory of the LORD settled on Mount Sinai, and the cloud covered it six days.

The seventh day He called to Moshe out of the midst of the cloud. The appearance of the glory of the LORD was like devouring fire on the top of the mountain in the eyes of the children of Yisra'el.

Moshe entered into the midst of the cloud, and went up on the mountain; and Moshe was on the mountain forty days and forty nights.

Haftarah

Jeremiah 33:25-26

Thus says the LORD: If My covenant of day and night fails, if I have not appointed the ordinances of heaven and earth; then will I also cast away the seed of Ya`akov, and of David My servant, so that I will not take of his seed to be rulers over the seed of Avraham, Yitzchak, and Ya`akov: for I will cause their captivity to return, and will have mercy on them.

Brit Chadasha

Mark 7:1-23

Then the Perushim, and some of the scribes gathered together to Him, having come from Yerushalayim. Now when they saw some of His talmidim eating bread with defiled, that is, unwashed, hands, they found fault. (For the Perushim, and all the Judeans, don't eat unless they wash their hands and forearms, holding to the tradition of the elders.

Parashat Mishpatim

Day 7

They don't eat when they come from the marketplace, unless they bathe themselves, and there are many other things, which they have received to hold to: washings of cups, pitchers, bronze vessels, and couches.)

The Perushim and the scribes asked Him, "Why don't Your talmidim walk according to the tradition of the elders, but eat their bread with unwashed hands?"

He answered them, "Well did Yeshaiyahu prophesy of you hypocrites, as it is written, 'This people honors Me with their lips, but their heart is far from Me. But in vain do they worship Me, teaching as doctrines the mitzvot of men.'"

For you set aside the mitzvah of God, and hold tightly to the tradition of men—the washing of pitchers and cups, and you do many other such things." He said to them, "Full well do you reject the mitzvah of God, that you may keep your tradition.

For Moshe said, 'Honor your father and your mother;' and, 'He who speaks evil of father or mother, let him be put to death.' But you say, 'If a man tells his father or his mother, "Whatever profit you might have received from me is korban, that is to say, given to God;"' then you no longer allow him to do anything for his father or his mother, making void the word of God by your tradition, which you have handed down. You do many things like this."

He called all the multitude to Himself, and said to them, "Hear Me, all of you, and understand. There is nothing from outside of the man, that going into him can defile him; but the things which proceed out of the man are those that defile the man. If anyone has ears to hear, let him hear!"

When He had entered into a house away from the multitude, His talmidim asked Him about the parable. He said to them, "Are you thus without understanding also? Don't you perceive that whatever goes into the man from outside can't defile him, because it doesn't go into his heart, but into his stomach, then into the latrine, thus making all foods clean?"

He said, "That which proceeds out of the man, that defiles the man. For from within, out of the hearts of men, proceed evil thoughts, adulteries, sexual sins, murders, thefts, covetings, wickedness, deceit, lustful desires, an evil eye, blasphemy, pride, and foolishness. All these evil things come from within, and defile the man."

Parashat: Terumah - "Offerings"

Daily Portion: Sunday

Exodus 25:1-20

The LORD spoke to Moshe, saying, "Speak to the children of Yisra'el, that they take an offering for Me. From everyone whose heart makes him willing you shall take my offering.

This is the offering which you shall take from them: gold, silver, brass, blue, purple, scarlet, fine linen, goats' hair, rams' skins dyed red, sea cow hides, shittim wood, oil for the light, spices for the anointing oil and for the sweet incense, shoham stones, and stones to be set for the efod and for the breastplate.

Let them make Me a sanctuary, that I may dwell among them. According to all that I show you, the pattern of the tent, and the pattern of all of its furniture, even so you shall make it. "They shall make a teivah of shittim wood.

Its length shall be two and a half cubits, its breadth a cubit and a half, and a cubit and a half its height. You shall overlay it with pure gold.

Inside and outside shall you overlay it, and shall make a gold molding around it. You shall cast four rings of gold for it, and put them in its four feet.

Two rings shall be on the one side of it, and two rings on the other side of it. You shall make poles of shittim wood, and overlay them with gold.

You shall put the poles into the rings on the sides of the ark to carry the ark. The poles shall be in the rings of the ark.

They shall not be taken from it. You shall put the testimony which I shall give you into the teivah. You shall make a mercy seat of pure gold.

Two and a half cubits shall be its length, and a cubit and a half its breadth. You shall make two Keruvim of hammered gold.

You shall make them at the two ends of the mercy seat. Make one Keruv at the one end, and one Keruv at the other end.

You shall make the Keruvim on its two ends of one piece with the mercy seat.

The Keruvim shall spread out their wings upward, covering the mercy seat with their wings, with their faces toward one another.

The faces of the Keruvim shall be toward the mercy seat.

Haftarah

1Kings 5:12-14

Parashat Terumah — Day 1

The LORD gave Shlomo wisdom, as He promised him; and there was shalom between Chiram and Shlomo; and they two made a league together.

King Shlomo raised a levy out of all Yisra'el; and the levy was thirty thousand men. He sent them to Levanon, ten thousand a month by courses; a month they were in Levanon, and two months at home; and Adoniram was over the men subject to forced labor.

Brit Chadasha

Hebrews 8:1-5

Now in the things which we are saying, the main point is this. We have such a Kohen Gadol, who sat down on the right hand of the throne of the Majesty in the heavens, a Servant of the sanctuary, and of the true tabernacle, which the Lord pitched, not man.

For every Kohen Gadol is appointed to offer both gifts and sacrifices. Therefore it is necessary that this Kohen Gadol also have something to offer.

For if He were on earth, He would not be a Kohen at all, seeing there are Kohanim who offer the gifts according to the Torah; who serve a copy and shadow of the heavenly things, even as Moshe was warned by God when he was about to make the tabernacle, for he said, "See, you shall make everything according to the pattern that was shown to you on the mountain."

Haftarah Note:

Most Messianic/Hebrew Bible translations render 1Kings 5:12-6:13 as 1Kings 5:26-6:13.

Parashat: Terumah - "Offerings"

Daily Portion: Monday

Exodus 25:21-35

You shall put the mercy seat on top of the ark, and in the ark you shall put the testimony that I will give you.

There I will meet with you, and I will tell you from above the mercy seat, from between the two Keruvim which are on the ark of the testimony, all that I command you for the children of Yisra'el.

"You shall make a table of shittim wood. Two cubits shall be its length, and a cubit its breadth, and one and a half cubits its height.

You shall overlay it with pure gold, and make a gold molding around it. You shall make a rim of a handbreadth around it. You shall make a golden molding on its rim around it.

You shall make four rings of gold for it, and put the rings in the four corners that are on its four feet. the rings shall be close to the rim, for places for the poles to carry the table.

You shall make the poles of shittim wood, and overlay them with gold, that the table may be carried with them.

You shall make its dishes, its spoons, its ladles, and its bowls to pour out offerings with. Of pure gold shall you make them. You shall set bread of the presence on the table before me always.

"You shall make a menorah of pure gold. Of hammered work shall the menorah be made, even its base, its shaft, its cups, its buds, and its flowers, shall be of one piece with it.

There shall be six branches going out of its sides: three branches of the menorah out of its one side, and three branches of the menorah out of its other side; three cups made like almond blossoms in one branch, a bud and a flower; and three cups made like almond blossoms in the other branch, a bud and a flower, so for the six branches going out of the menorah; and in the menorah four cups made like almond blossoms, its buds and its flowers; and a bud under two branches of one piece with it, and a bud under two branches of one piece with it, and a bud under two branches of one piece with it, for the six branches going out of the menorah.

Haftarah

1Kings 5:15-18

Parashat Terumah — Day 2

Shlomo had seventy thousand who bore burdens, and eighty thousand who were stone cutters in the mountains; besides Shlomo's chief officers who were over the work, three thousand and three hundred, who bore rule over the people who labored in the work.

The king commanded, and they hewed out great stones, costly stones, to lay the foundation of the house with worked stone.

Shlomo's builders and Chiram's builders and the Givli did fashion them, and prepared the timber and the stones to build the house.

Brit Chadasha

Hebrews 8:6-9

But now He has obtained a more excellent ministry, by so much as He is also the mediator of a better covenant, which has been enacted on better promises.

For if that first covenant had been faultless, then no place would have been sought for a second.

For finding fault with them, He said, "Behold, the days come," says the Lord, "that I will make a new covenant with the house of Yisra'el and with the house of Yehudah; not according to the covenant that I made with their fathers, in the day that I took them by the hand to lead them out of the land of Egypt; for they didn't continue in My covenant, and I disregarded them," says the Lord.

Parashat: Terumah - "Offerings"

Daily Portion: Tuesday

Exodus 25:36-26:10

Their buds and their branches shall be of one piece with it, the whole of it one beaten work of pure gold.

You shall make its lamps seven, and they shall light its lamps to give light to the space in front of it. Its snuffers and its snuff dishes shall be of pure gold.

It shall be made of a talent of pure gold, with all these accessories. See that you make them after their pattern, which has been shown to you on the mountain.

"Moreover you shall make the tent with ten curtains; of fine twined linen, and blue, and purple, and scarlet, with Keruvim. The work of the skillful workman you shall make them.

The length of each curtain shall be twenty-eight cubits, and the breadth of each curtain four cubits: all the curtains shall have one measure.

Five curtains shall be coupled together one to another; and the other five curtains shall be coupled one to another.

You shall make loops of blue on the edge of the one curtain from the edge in the coupling; and likewise shall you make in the edge of the curtain that is outmost in the second coupling.

You shall make fifty loops in the one curtain, and you shall make fifty loops in the edge of the curtain that is in the second coupling. The loops shall be opposite one to another.

You shall make fifty clasps of gold, and couple the curtains one to another with the clasps: and the tent shall be a unit. "You shall make curtains of goats' hair for a covering over the tent: eleven curtains shall you make them.

The length of each curtain shall be thirty cubits, and the breadth of each curtain four cubits: the eleven curtains shall have one measure. You shall couple five curtains by themselves, and six curtains by themselves, and shall double over the sixth curtain in the forefront of the tent.

You shall make fifty loops on the edge of the one curtain that is outmost in the coupling, and fifty loops on the edge of the curtain which is outmost in the second coupling.

Haftarah

1Kings 6:1-2

It happened in the four hundred and eightieth year after the children of Yisra'el were come out of the land of Egypt, in the fourth year of Shlomo's reign over Yisra'el, in the month Ziv, which is the second month, that he began to build the house of the LORD.

The house which king Shlomo built for the LORD, the length of it was sixty cubits, and the breadth of it twenty [cubits], and the height of it thirty cubits.

Parashat Terumah — Day 3

Brit Chadasha

Hebrews 8:10-12

"For this is the covenant that I will make with the house of Yisra'el.

After those days," says the Lord, "I will put My laws into their mind, I will also write them on their heart.

I will be to them a God, and they will be to Me a people.

They will not teach every man his fellow citizen, and every man his brother, saying, 'Know the Lord,' for all will know Me, from the least of them to the greatest of them.

For I will be merciful to their unrighteousness. I will remember their sins and lawless deeds no more."

Parashat: Terumah - "Offerings"

Daily Portion: Wednesday

Exodus 26:11-25

You shall make fifty clasps of brass, and put the clasps into the loops, and couple the tent together, that it may be one.

The overhanging part that remains of the curtains of the tent, the half curtain that remains, shall hang over the back of the tent.

The cubit on the one side, and the cubit on the other side, of that which remains in the length of the curtains of the tent, shall hang over the sides of the tent on this side and on that side, to cover it.

You shall make a covering for the tent of rams' skins dyed red, and a covering of sea cow hides above.

"You shall make the boards for the tent of shittim wood, standing up. Ten cubits shall be the length of a board, and one and a half cubits the breadth of each board.

There shall be two tenons in each board, joined to one another: thus shall you make for all the boards of the tent.

You shall make the boards for the tent, twenty boards for the south side southward.

You shall make forty sockets of silver under the twenty boards; two sockets under one board for its two tenons, and two sockets under another board for its two tenons.

For the second side of the tent, on the north side, twenty boards, and their forty sockets of silver; two sockets under one board, and two sockets under another board.

For the far part of the tent westward you shall make six boards. Two boards shall you make for the corners of the tent in the far part.

They shall be double beneath, and in like manner they shall be entire to the top of it to one ring: thus shall it be for them both; they shall be for the two corners.

There shall be eight boards, and their sockets of silver, sixteen sockets; two sockets under one board, and two sockets under another board.

Haftarah

1 Kings 6:3-6

Parashat Terumah — Day 4

The porch before the temple of the house, twenty cubits was the length of it, according to the breadth of the house; [and] ten cubits was the breadth of it before the house.

For the house he made windows of fixed lattice work.

Against the wall of the house he built stories round about, against the walls of the house round about, both of the temple and of the oracle; and he made side chambers round about.

The nethermost story was five cubits broad, and the middle was six cubits broad, and the third was seven cubits broad; for on the outside he made offsets [in the wall] of the house round about, that [the beams] should not have hold in the walls of the house.

Brit Chadasha

Hebrews 8:13-9:2

In that He says, "A new covenant," He has made the first old.

But that which is becoming old and grows aged is near to vanishing away.

Now indeed even the first covenant had ordinances of divine service, and an earthly sanctuary.

For a tabernacle was prepared.

In the first part were the menorah, the table, and the show bread; which is called the Holy Place.

Parashat: Terumah - "Offerings"

Daily Portion: Thursday

Exodus 26:26-27:2

"You shall make bars of shittim wood: five for the boards of the one side of the tent, and five bars for the boards of the other side of the tent, and five bars for the boards of the side of the tent, for the far part westward.

The middle bar in the midst of the boards shall pass through from end to end. You shall overlay the boards with gold, and make their rings of gold for places for the bars: and you shall overlay the bars with gold.

You shall set up the tent according to the way that it was shown to you on the mountain.

"You shall make a veil of blue, and purple, and scarlet, and fine twined linen, with Keruvim. The work of the skillful workman shall it be made.

You shall hang it on four pillars of shittim overlaid with gold; their hooks shall be of gold, on four sockets of silver.

You shall hang up the veil under the clasps, and shall bring the ark of the testimony in there within the veil: and the veil shall separate the holy place from the most holy for you.

You shall put the mercy seat on the ark of the testimony in the most holy place.

You shall set the table outside the veil, and the menorah over against the table on the side of the tent toward the south: and you shall put the table on the north side.

"You shall make a screen for the door of the Tent, of blue, and purple, and scarlet, and fine twined linen, the work of the embroiderer.

You shall make for the screen five pillars of shittim, and overlay them with gold: their hooks shall be of gold: and you shall cast five sockets of brass for them.

"You shall make the altar of shittim wood, five cubits long, and five cubits broad; the altar shall be foursquare: and its height shall be three cubits.

You shall make its horns on its four corners; its horns shall be of one piece with it; and you shall overlay it with brass.

Haftarah

1Kings 6:7-9

Parashat Terumah — Day 5

The house, when it was in building, was built of stone made ready at the quarry; and there was neither hammer nor axe nor any tool of iron heard in the house, while it was in building.

The door for the middle side chambers was in the right side of the house: and they went up by winding stairs into the middle [story], and out of the middle into the third.

So he built the house, and finished it; and he covered the house with beams and planks of cedar.

Brit Chadasha

Hebrews 9:3-5

After the second veil was the tabernacle which is called the Holy of Holies, having a golden altar of incense, and the ark of the covenant overlaid on all sides with gold, in which was a golden pot holding the manna, Aharon's rod that budded, and the tablets of the covenant; and above it Keruvim of glory overshadowing the mercy seat, of which things we can't speak now in detail.

Parashat: Terumah - "Offerings"

Daily Portion: Friday

Exodus 27:3-19

You shall make its pots to take away its ashes, its shovels, its basins, its flesh hooks, and its fire pans: all its vessels you shall make of brass.

You shall make a grating for it of network of brass: and on the net you shall make four bronze rings in its four corners.

You shall put it under the ledge around the altar beneath, that the net may reach halfway up the altar. You shall make poles for the altar, poles of shittim wood, and overlay them with brass.

Its poles shall be put into the rings, and the poles shall be on the two sides of the altar, when carrying it. Hollow with planks shall you make it: as it has been shown you on the mountain, so shall they make it.

"You shall make the court of the tent: for the south side southward there shall be hangings for the court of fine twined linen one hundred cubits long for one side: and the pillars of it shall be twenty, and their sockets twenty, of brass; the hooks of the pillars and their fillets shall be of silver.

Likewise for the north side in length there shall be hangings one hundred cubits long, and the pillars of it twenty, and their sockets twenty, of brass; the hooks of the pillars, and their fillets, of silver.

For the breadth of the court on the west side shall be hangings of fifty cubits; their pillars ten, and their sockets ten. The breadth of the court on the east side eastward shall be fifty cubits.

The hangings for the one side of the gate shall be fifteen cubits; their pillars three, and their sockets three. For the other side shall be hangings of fifteen cubits; their pillars three, and their sockets three.

For the gate of the court shall be a screen of twenty cubits, of blue, and purple, and scarlet, and fine twined linen, the work of the embroiderer; their pillars four, and their sockets four. All the pillars of the court round about shall be filleted with silver; their hooks of silver, and their sockets of brass.

The length of the court shall be one hundred cubits, and the breadth fifty every where, and the height five cubits, of fine twined linen, and their sockets of brass. All the instruments of the tent in all its service, and all the pins of it, and all the pins of the court, shall be of brass.

Haftarah

1Kings 6:10-13

He built the stories against all the house, each five cubits high: and they rested on the house with timber of cedar.

The word of the LORD came to Shlomo, saying, Concerning this house which you are building, if you will walk in my statutes, and execute my ordinances, and keep all my mitzvot to walk in them; then will I establish my word with you, which I spoke to David your father.

I will dwell among the children of Yisra'el, and will not forsake my people Yisra'el.

Parashat Terumah — Day 6

Brit Chadasha

Hebrews 9:23-24; 10:1

It was necessary therefore that the copies of the things in the heavens should be cleansed with these; but the heavenly things themselves with better sacrifices than these.

For Messiah hasn't entered into holy places made with hands, which are representations of the true, but into heaven itself, now to appear in the presence of God for us; For the Torah, having a shadow of the good to come, not the very image of the things, can never with the same sacrifices year by year, which they offer continually, make perfect those who draw near.

Parashat Terumah — Day 7

Special Shabbat Readings

Daily Portion: Shabbat

Isaiah 66:1-24

Thus says the LORD, heaven is My throne, and the earth is My footstool: what manner of house will you build to Me? and what place shall be My rest?

For all these things has My hand made, and [so] all these things came to be, says the LORD: but to this man will I look, even to him who is poor and of a contrite spirit, and who trembles at My word.

He who kills an ox is as he who kills a man; he who sacrifices a lamb, as he who breaks a dog's neck; he who offers an offering, [as he who offers] pig's blood; he who burns frankincense, as he who blesses an idol.

Yes, they have chosen their own ways, and their soul delights in their abominations: I also will choose their delusions, and will bring their fears on them; because when I called, none did answer; when I spoke, they did not hear: but they did that which was evil in My eyes, and chose that in which I didn't delight.

Hear the word of the LORD, you who tremble at His word: Your brothers who hate you, who cast you out for My name's sake, have said, Let the LORD be glorified, that we may see your joy; but it is those who shall be disappointed.

A voice of tumult from the city, a voice from the temple, a voice of the LORD that renders recompense to His enemies. Before she travailed, she brought forth; before her pain came, she was delivered of a boy.

Who has heard such a thing? who has seen such things? Shall a land be born in one day? shall a nation be brought forth at once? for as soon as Tziyon travailed, she brought forth her children.

Shall I bring to the birth, and not cause to bring forth? says the LORD; shall I who cause to bring forth shut [the womb]? says your God.

Rejoice you with Yerushalayim, and be glad for her, all you who love her: rejoice for joy with her, all you who mourn over her; that you may suck and be satisfied with the breasts of her consolations; that you may milk out, and be delighted with the abundance of her glory.

For thus says the LORD, Behold, I will extend shalom to her like a river, and the glory of the nations like an overflowing stream: and you shall suck [of it]; you shall be borne on the side, and shall be dandled on the knees.

As one whom his mother comforts, so will I comfort you; and you shall be comforted in Yerushalayim. You shall see [it], and your heart shall rejoice, and your bones shall flourish like the tender grass: and the hand of the LORD shall be known toward His servants; and He will have indignation against His enemies.

Parashat Terumah

Day 7

For, behold, the LORD will come with fire, and His chariots shall be like the whirlwind; to render His anger with fierceness, and His rebuke with flames of fire.

For by fire will the LORD execute judgment, and by His sword, on all flesh; and the slain of the LORD shall be many.

Those who sanctify themselves and purify themselves [to go] to the gardens, behind one in the midst, eating pig's flesh, and the abomination, and the akbar, they shall come to an end together, says the LORD.

For I [know] their works and their thoughts: [the time] comes, that I will gather all nations and languages; and they shall come, and shall see my glory.

I will set a sign among them, and I will send such as escape of them to the nations, to Tarshish, Pul, and Lud, who draw the bow, to Tuval and Yavan, to the islands afar off, who have not heard My fame, neither have seen My glory; and they shall declare My glory among the nations.

They shall bring all your brothers out of all the nations for an offering to the LORD, on horses, and in chariots, and in litters, and on mules, and on dromedaries, to My holy mountain Yerushalayim, says the LORD, as the children of Yisra'el bring their offering in a clean vessel into the house of the LORD.

Of them also will I take for Kohanim [and] for Levites, says the LORD. For as the new heavens and the new earth, which I will make, shall remain before Me, says the LORD, so shall your seed and your name remain.

It shall happen, that from one new moon to another, and from one Shabbat to another, shall all flesh come to worship before Me, says the LORD.

They shall go forth, and look on the dead bodies of the men who have transgressed against Me: for their worm shall not die, neither shall their fire be quenched; and they shall be an abhorring to all flesh.

Parashat: Tetzaveh - "You Shall Command"

Daily Portion: Sunday

Exodus 27:20-28:11

"You shall command the children of Yisra'el, that they bring to you pure olive oil beaten for the light, to cause a lamp to burn continually.

In the tent of meeting, outside the veil which is before the testimony, Aharon and his sons shall keep it in order from evening to morning before the LORD: it shall be a statute forever throughout their generations on the behalf of the children of Yisra'el."

Bring Aharon your brother, and his sons with him, near to you from among the children of Yisra'el, that he may minister to Me in the Kohen's office, even Aharon, Nadav and Avihu, El`azar and Itamar, Aharon's sons.

You shall make holy garments for Aharon your brother, for glory and for beauty. You shall speak to all who are wise-hearted, whom I have filled with the spirit of wisdom, that they make Aharon's garments to sanctify him, that he may minister to Me in the Kohen's office.

These are the garments which they shall make: a breastplate, and an efod, and a robe, and a coat of checker work, a turban, and a sash: and they shall make holy garments for Aharon your brother, and his sons, that he may minister to Me in the Kohen's office.

They shall take the gold, and the blue, and the purple, and the scarlet, and the fine linen. "They shall make the efod of gold, of blue, and purple, scarlet, and fine twined linen, the work of the skillful workman. It shall have two shoulder straps joined to the two ends of it, that it may be joined together.

The skillfully woven band, which is on it, that is on him, shall be like its work and of the same piece; of gold, of blue, and purple, and scarlet, and fine twined linen.

You shall take two shoham stones, and engrave on them the names of the children of Yisra'el: six of their names on the one stone, and the names of the six that remain on the other stone, in the order of their birth.

With the work of an engraver in stone, like the engravings of a signet, shall you engrave the two stones, according to the names of the children of Yisra'el: you shall make them to be enclosed in settings of gold.

Haftarah

Ezekiel 43:10-11

Parashat Tetzaveh — Day 1

You, son of man, show the house to the house of Yisra'el, that they may be ashamed of their iniquities; and let them measure the pattern.

If they be ashamed of all that they have done, make known to them the form of the house, and the fashion of it, and the exits of it, and the entrances of it, and all the forms of it, and all the ordinances of it, and all the forms of it, and all the laws of it; and write it in their sight; that they may keep the whole form of it, and all the ordinances of it, and do them.

Brit Chadasha

Romans 12:1-5

Therefore I urge you, brothers, by the mercies of God, to present your bodies a living sacrifice, holy, acceptable to God, which is your spiritual service.

Don't be conformed to this world, but be transformed by the renewing of your mind, so that you may prove what is the good, well-pleasing, and perfect will of God.

For I say, through the grace that was given me, to every man who is among you, not to think of himself more highly than he ought to think; but to think reasonably, as God has apportioned to each person a measure of faith.

For even as we have many members in one body, and all the members don't have the same function, so we, who are many, are one body in Messiah, and individually members one of another.

Parashat: Tetzaveh - "You Shall Command"

Daily Portion: Monday

Exodus 28:12-28

You shall put the two stones on the shoulder straps of the efod, to be stones of memorial for the children of Yisra'el: and Aharon shall bear their names before the LORD on his two shoulders for a memorial.

You shall make settings of gold, and two chains of pure gold; you shall make them like cords of braided work: and you shall put the braided chains on the settings. "You shall make a breastplate of judgment, the work of the skillful workman; like the work of the efod you shall make it; of gold, of blue, and purple, and scarlet, and fine twined linen, shall you make it.

It shall be square and folded double; a span shall be its length of it, and a span its breadth. You shall set in it settings of stones, four rows of stones: a row of odem, pitdah, and bareket shall be the first row; and the second row a nofek, a sappir, and an yahalom; and the third row a lehshem, an shebu, and an akhlamah; and the fourth row a tarshish, an shoham, and a yashefay: they shall be enclosed in gold in their settings.

The stones shall be according to the names of the children of Yisra'el, twelve, according to their names; like the engravings of a signet, everyone according to his name, they shall be for the twelve tribes. You shall make on the breastplate chains like cords, of braided work of pure gold.

You shall make on the breastplate two rings of gold, and shall put the two rings on the two ends of the breastplate. You shall put the two braided chains of gold in the two rings at the ends of the breastplate. The other two ends of the two braided chains you shall put on the two settings, and put them on the shoulder straps of the efod in the forepart of it.

You shall make two rings of gold, and you shall put them on the two ends of the breastplate, on its edge, which is toward the side of the efod inward. You shall make two rings of gold, and shall put them on the two shoulder straps of the efod underneath, in the forepart of it, close by the coupling of it, above the skillfully woven band of the efod.

They shall bind the breastplate by the rings of it to the rings of the efod with a lace of blue, that it may be on the skillfully woven band of the efod, and that the breastplate may not swing out from the efod.

Haftarah

Ezekiel 43:12-13

This is the law of the house: on the top of the mountain the whole limit of it round about shall be most holy.

Behold, this is the law of the house.

These are the measures of the altar by cubits (the cubit is a cubit and a handbreadth): the bottom shall be a cubit, and the breadth a cubit, and the border of it by the edge of it round about a span; and this shall be the base of the altar.

Parashat Tetzaveh — Day 2

Brit Chadasha

Romans 12:6-13

Having gifts differing according to the grace that was given to us, if prophecy, let us prophesy according to the proportion of our faith; or service, let us give ourselves to service; or he who teaches, to his teaching; or he who exhorts, to his exhorting: he who gives, let him do it with liberality; he who rules, with diligence; he who shows mercy, with cheerfulness.

Let love be without hypocrisy.

Abhor that which is evil.

Cling to that which is good.

In love of the brothers be tenderly affectionate one to another; in honor preferring one another; not lagging in diligence; fervent in spirit; serving the Lord; rejoicing in hope; enduring in troubles; continuing steadfastly in prayer; contributing to the needs of the holy ones; given to hospitality.

Parashat: Tetzaveh - "You Shall Command"

Daily Portion: Tuesday

Exodus 28:29-41

Aharon shall bear the names of the children of Yisra'el in the breastplate of judgment on his heart, when he goes in to the holy place, for a memorial before the LORD continually.

You shall put in the breastplate of judgment the Urim and the Tummim; and they shall be on Aharon's heart, when he goes in before the LORD: and Aharon shall bear the judgment of the children of Yisra'el on his heart before the LORD continually."

You shall make the robe of the efod all of blue. It shall have a hole for the head in the midst of it: it shall have a binding of woven work round about the hole of it, as it were the hole of a coat of mail, that it not be torn.

On its tzitzit you shall make pomegranates of blue, and of purple, and of scarlet, around its tzitzit; and bells of gold between them round about: a golden bell and a pomegranate, a golden bell and a pomegranate, on the tzitzit of the robe round about.

It shall be on Aharon to minister: and the sound of it shall be heard when he goes in to the holy place before the LORD, and when he comes out, that he not die. "You shall make a plate of pure gold, and engrave on it, like the engravings of a signet, 'HOLY TO THE LORD.'

You shall put it on a lace of blue, and it shall be on the sash; on the front of the sash it shall be. It shall be on Aharon's forehead, and Aharon shall bear the iniquity of the holy things, which the children of Yisra'el shall make holy in all their holy gifts; and it shall be always on his forehead, that they may be accepted before the LORD.

You shall weave the coat in checker work of fine linen, and you shall make a turban of fine linen, and you shall make a sash, the work of the embroiderer.

"You shall make coats for Aharon's sons, and you shall make sashes for them and headbands shall you make for them, for glory and for beauty.

You shall put them on Aharon your brother, and on his sons with him, and shall anoint them, and consecrate them, and sanctify them, that they may minister to Me in the Kohen's office.

Haftarah

Ezekiel 43:14-17

Parashat Tetzaveh — Day 3

From the bottom on the ground to the lower ledge shall be two cubits, and the breadth one cubit; and from the lesser ledge to the greater ledge shall be four cubits, and the breadth a cubit.

The upper altar shall be four cubits; and from the altar hearth and upward there shall be four horns.

The altar hearth shall be twelve [cubits] long by twelve broad, square in the four sides of it.

The ledge shall be fourteen [cubits] long by fourteen broad in the four sides of it; and the border about it shall be half a cubit; and the bottom of it shall be a cubit round about; and the steps of it shall look toward the east.

Brit Chadasha

Romans 12:14-21

Bless those who persecute you; bless, and don't curse. Rejoice with those who rejoice.

Weep with those who weep. Be of the same mind one toward another.

Don't set your mind on high things, but associate with the humble.

Don't be wise in your own conceits.

Repay no one evil for evil.

Respect what is honorable in the sight of all men.

If it is possible, as much as it is up to you, be at peace with all men.

Don't seek revenge yourselves, beloved, but give place to God's wrath. For it is written, "Vengeance belongs to me; I will repay, says the Lord."

Therefore "If your enemy is hungry, feed him. If he is thirsty, give him a drink; for in doing so, you will heap coals of fire on his head."

Don't be overcome by evil, but overcome evil with good.

Parashat: Tetzaveh - "You Shall Command"

Daily Portion: Wednesday

Exodus 28:42-29:14

You shall make them linen breeches to cover the flesh of their nakedness; from the waist even to the thighs they shall reach: They shall be on Aharon, and on his sons, when they go in to the tent of meeting, or when they come near to the altar to minister in the holy place; that they don't bear iniquity, and die: it shall be a statute forever to him and to his descendants after him."

This is the thing that you shall do to them to make them holy, to minister to me in the Kohen's office: take one young bull and two rams without blemish, matzah, unleavened cakes mixed with oil, and unleavened wafers anointed with oil: you shall make them of fine wheat flour.

You shall put them into one basket, and bring them in the basket, with the bull and the two rams.

You shall bring Aharon and his sons to the door of the tent of meeting, and shall wash them with water.

You shall take the garments, and put on Aharon the coat, the robe of the efod, the efod, and the breastplate, and dress him with the skillfully woven band of the efod; and you shall set the turban on his head, and put the holy crown on the turban.

Then you shall take the anointing oil, and pour it on his head, and anoint him. You shall bring his sons, and put coats on them. You shall dress them with belts, Aharon and his sons, and bind headbands on them: and they shall have the priesthood by a perpetual statute: and you shall consecrate Aharon and his sons.

"You shall bring the bull before the tent of meeting: and Aharon and his sons shall lay their hands on the head of the bull. You shall kill the bull before the LORD, at the door of the tent of meeting.

You shall take of the blood of the bull, and put it on the horns of the altar with your finger; and you shall pour out all the blood at the base of the altar.

You shall take all the fat that covers the innards, the cover of the liver, the two kidneys, and the fat that is on them, and burn them on the altar.

But the flesh of the bull, and its skin, and its dung, you shall burn with fire outside of the camp: it is a sin offering.

Haftarah

Ezekiel 43:18-19

Parashat Tetzaveh — Day 4

He said to me, Son of man, thus says the Lord GOD: These are the ordinances of the altar in the day when they shall make it, to offer burnt offerings thereon, and to sprinkle blood thereon.

You shall give to the Kohanim the Levites who are of the seed of Tzadok, who are near to me, to minister to me, says the Lord GOD, a young bull for a sin offering.

Brit Chadasha

Romans 13:1-7

Let every soul be in subjection to the higher authorities, for there is no authority except from God, and those who exist are ordained by God.

Therefore he who resists the authority, withstands the ordinance of God; and those who withstand will receive to themselves judgment.

For rulers are not a terror to the good work, but to the evil.

Do you desire to have no fear of the authority?

Do that which is good, and you will have praise from the same, for he is a servant of God to you for good.

But if you do that which is evil, be afraid, for he doesn't bear the sword in vain; for he is a servant of God, an avenger for wrath to him who does evil.

Therefore you need to be in subjection, not only because of the wrath, but also for conscience' sake.

For this reason you also pay taxes, for they are servants of God's service, attending continually on this very thing.

Give therefore to everyone what you owe: taxes to whom taxes are due; customs to whom customs; respect to whom respect; honor to whom honor.

Parashat: Tetzaveh - "You Shall Command"

Daily Portion: Thursday

Exodus 29:15-28

"You shall also take the one ram; and Aharon and his sons shall lay their hands on the head of the ram.

You shall kill the ram, and you shall take its blood, and sprinkle it around on the altar.

You shall cut the ram into its pieces, and wash its innards, and its legs, and put them with its pieces, and with its head.

You shall burn the whole ram on the altar: it is a burnt offering to the LORD; it is a sweet savor, an offering made by fire to the LORD."

You shall take the other ram; and Aharon and his sons shall lay their hands on the head of the ram.

Then you shall kill the ram, and take some of its blood, and put it on the tip of the right ear of Aharon, and on the tip of the right ear of his sons, and on the thumb of their right hand, and on the big toe of their right foot, and sprinkle the blood on the altar round about.

You shall take of the blood that is on the altar, and of the anointing oil, and sprinkle it on Aharon, and on his garments, and on his sons, and on the garments of his sons with him: and he shall be made holy, and his garments, and his sons, and his sons' garments with him.

Also you shall take some of the ram's fat, the fat tail, the fat that covers the innards, the cover of the liver, the two kidneys, the fat that is on them, and the right thigh (for it is a ram of consecration), and one loaf of bread, one cake of oiled bread, and one wafer out of the basket of matzah that is before the LORD.

You shall put all of this in Aharon's hands, and in his sons' hands, and shall wave them for a wave offering before the LORD.

You shall take them from their hands, and burn them on the altar on the burnt offering, for a sweet savor before the LORD: it is an offering made by fire to the LORD.

"You shall take the breast of Aharon's ram of consecration, and wave it for a wave offering before the LORD: and it shall be your portion.

You shall sanctify the breast of the wave offering, and the thigh of the wave offering, which is waved, and which is heaved up, of the ram of consecration, even of that which is for Aharon, and of that which is for his sons: and it shall be for Aharon and his sons as their portion forever from the children of Yisra'el; for it is a wave offering: and it shall be a wave offering from the children of Yisra'el of the sacrifices of their shalom offerings, even their wave offering to the LORD.

Parashat Tetzaveh — Day 5

Haftarah

Ezekiel 43:20-21

You shall take of the blood of it, and put it on the four horns of it, and on the four corners of the ledge, and on the border round about: thus shall you cleanse it and make atonement for it.

You shall also take the bull of the sin offering, and it shall be burnt in the appointed place of the house, outside of the sanctuary.

Brit Chadasha

Romans 13:8-10

Owe no one anything, except to love one another; for he who loves his neighbor has fulfilled the law.

For the mitzvot, "You shall not commit adultery," "You shall not murder," "You shall not steal," "You shall not give false testimony," "You shall not covet," and whatever other mitzvot there are, are all summed up in this saying, namely, "You shall love your neighbor as yourself."

Love doesn't harm a neighbor. Love therefore is the fulfillment of the law.

Parashat Tetzaveh Day 6

Parashat: Tetzaveh - "You Shall Command"

Daily Portion: Friday

Exodus 29:29-41

"The holy garments of Aharon shall be for his sons after him, to be anointed in them, and to be consecrated in them. Seven days shall the son who is Kohen in his place put them on, when he comes into the tent of meeting to minister in the holy place."

You shall take the ram of consecration, and boil its flesh in a holy place. Aharon and his sons shall eat the flesh of the ram, and the bread that is in the basket, at the door of the tent of meeting.

They shall eat those things with which atonement was made, to consecrate and sanctify them: but a stranger shall not eat of it, because they are holy.

If anything of the flesh of the consecration, or of the bread, remains to the morning, then you shall burn the remainder with fire: it shall not be eaten, because it is holy.

"Thus shall you do to Aharon, and to his sons, according to all that I have commanded you. Seven days shall you consecrate them.

Every day shall you offer the bull of sin offering for atonement: and you shall cleanse the altar, when you make atonement for it; and you shall anoint it, to sanctify it.

Seven days you shall make atonement for the altar, and sanctify it: and the altar shall be most holy; whatever touches the altar shall be holy."

Now this is that which you shall offer on the altar: two lambs a year old day by day continually.

The one lamb you shall offer in the morning; and the other lamb you shall offer at evening: and with the one lamb a tenth part of an efah of fine flour mixed with the fourth part of a hin of beaten oil, and the fourth part of a hin of wine for a drink offering.

The other lamb you shall offer at evening, and shall do to it according to the meal offering of the morning, and according to its drink offering, for a sweet savor, an offering made by fire to the LORD.

Haftarah

Ezekiel 43:22-24

Parashat Tetzaveh — Day 6

On the second day you shall offer a male goat without blemish for a sin offering; and they shall cleanse the altar, as they did cleanse it with the bull.

When you have made an end of cleansing it, you shall offer a young bull without blemish, and a ram out of the flock without blemish.

You shall bring them near before the LORD, and the Kohanim shall cast salt on them, and they shall offer them up for a burnt offering to the LORD.

Brit Chadasha

Romans 13:11-14

Do this, knowing the time, that it is already time for you to awaken out of sleep, for salvation is now nearer to us than when we first believed.

The night is far gone, and the day is near.

Let's therefore throw off the works of darkness, and let's put on the armor of light.

Let us walk properly, as in the day; not in reveling and drunkenness, not in sexual promiscuity and lustful acts, and not in strife and jealousy.

But put on the Lord Yeshua the Messiah, and make no provision for the flesh, for its lusts.

Parashat: Tetzaveh - "You Shall Command"

Daily Portion: Shabbat

Exodus 29:42-30:10

It shall be a continual burnt offering throughout your generations at the door of the tent of meeting before the LORD, where I will meet with you, to speak there to you. There I will meet with the children of Yisra'el; and the place shall be sanctified by My glory.

I will sanctify the tent of meeting and the altar: Aharon also and his sons I will sanctify, to minister to Me in the Kohen's office.

I will dwell among the children of Yisra'el, and will be their God. They shall know that I am the LORD their God, who brought them forth out of the land of Egypt, that I might dwell among them: I am the LORD their God.

"You shall make an altar to burn incense on. You shall make it of shittim wood. Its length shall be a cubit, and its breadth a cubit. It shall be square, and its height shall be two cubits.

Its horns shall be of one piece with it. You shall overlay it with pure gold, the top of it, the sides of it around it, and its horns; and you shall make a gold molding around it.

You shall make two golden rings for it under its molding; on its two ribs, on its two sides you shall make them; and they shall be for places for poles with which to bear it.

You shall make the poles of shittim wood, and overlay them with gold. You shall put it before the veil that is by the ark of the testimony, before the mercy seat that is over the testimony, where I will meet with you.

Aharon shall burn incense of sweet spices on it every morning. When he tends the lamps, he shall burn it. When Aharon lights the lamps at evening, he shall burn it, a perpetual incense before the LORD throughout your generations.

You shall offer no strange incense on it, nor burnt offering, nor meal offering; and you shall pour no drink offering on it.

Aharon shall make atonement on its horns once in the year; with the blood of the sin offering of atonement once in the year he shall make atonement for it throughout your generations. It is most holy to the LORD."

Haftarah

Ezekiel 43:25-27

Seven days shall you prepare every day a goat for a sin offering: they shall also prepare a young bull, and a ram out of the flock, without blemish.

Seven days shall they make atonement for the altar and purify it; so shall they consecrate it.

When they have accomplished the days, it shall be that on the eighth day, and forward, the Kohanim shall make your burnt offerings on the altar, and your shalom offerings; and I will accept you, says the Lord GOD.

Parashat Tetzaveh

Day 7

Brit Chadasha

Philippians 4:10-20

But I rejoice in the Lord greatly, that now at length you have revived your thought for me; in which you did indeed take thought, but you lacked opportunity. Not that I speak in respect to lack, for I have learned in whatever state I am, to be content in it.

I know how to be humbled, and I know also how to abound. In everything and in all things I have learned the secret both to be filled and to be hungry, both to abound and to be in need. I can do all things through Messiah, who strengthens me. However you did well that you shared in my affliction.

You yourselves also know, you Philippians, that in the beginning of the Good News, when I departed from Macedonia, no assembly shared with me in the matter of giving and receiving but you only. For even in Thessalonica you sent once and again to my need.

Not that I seek for the gift, but I seek for the fruit that increases to your account. But I have all things, and abound. I am filled, having received from Epaphroditus the things that came from you, a sweet-smelling fragrance, an acceptable and well-pleasing sacrifice to God.

My God will supply every need of yours according to his riches in glory in Messiah Yeshua. Now to our God and Father be the glory forever and ever! Amein.

Parashat: Ki Tisa - "When You Elevate"

Daily Portion: Sunday

Exodus 30:11-33

The LORD spoke to Moshe, saying, "When you take a census of the children of Yisra'el, according to those who are numbered among them, then each man shall give a ransom for his soul to the LORD, when you number them; that there be no plague among them when you number them. They shall give this, everyone who passes over to those who are numbered, half a shekel after the shekel of the sanctuary; (the shekel is twenty gerahs;) half a shekel for an offering to the LORD. Everyone who passes over to those who are numbered, from twenty years old and upward, shall give the offering to the LORD. The rich shall not give more, and the poor shall not give less, than the half shekel, when they give the offering of the LORD, to make atonement for your souls. You shall take the atonement money from the children of Yisra'el, and shall appoint it for the service of the tent of meeting; that it may be a memorial for the children of Yisra'el before the LORD, to make atonement for your souls." The LORD spoke to Moshe, saying, "You shall also make a basin of brass, and the base of it of brass, in which to wash. You shall put it between the tent of meeting and the altar, and you shall put water in it. Aharon and his sons shall wash their hands and their feet in it. When they go into the tent of meeting, they shall wash with water, that they not die; or when they come near to the altar to minister, to burn an offering made by fire to the LORD. So they shall wash their hands and their feet, that they not die: and it shall be a statute forever to them, even to him and to his descendants throughout their generations." Moreover the LORD spoke to Moshe, saying, "Also take fine spices: of liquid myrrh, five hundred shekels; and of fragrant cinnamon half as much, even two hundred and fifty; and of fragrant cane, two hundred and fifty; and of cassia five hundred, after the shekel of the sanctuary; and a hin of olive oil. You shall make it a holy anointing oil, a perfume compounded after the art of the perfumer: it shall be a holy anointing oil. You shall use it to anoint the tent of meeting, the ark of the testimony, the table and all its articles, the menorah and its accessories, the altar of incense, the altar of burnt offering with all its utensils, and the basin with its base. You shall sanctify them, that they may be most holy. Whatever touches them shall be holy. You shall anoint Aharon and his sons, and sanctify them, that they may minister to Me in the Kohen's office. You shall speak to the children of Yisra'el, saying, 'This shall be a holy anointing oil to Me throughout your generations. It shall not be poured on man's flesh, neither shall you make any like it, according to its composition: it is holy. It shall be holy to you. Whoever compounds any like it, or whoever puts any of it on a stranger, he shall be cut off from his people.'"

Haftarah

1Kings 18:1-5

Parashat Ki Tisa — Day 1

It happened after many days, that the word of the LORD came to Eliyahu, in the third year, saying, Go, show yourself to Ach'av; and I will send rain on the earth.

Eliyahu went to show himself to Ach'av. The famine was sore in Shomron.

Ach'av called `Ovadyah 1, who was over the household. (Now `Ovadyah 1 feared the LORD greatly:

for it was so, when Izevel cut off the prophets of the LORD, that `Ovadyah 1 took one hundred prophets, and hid them by fifty in a cave, and fed them with bread and water.)

Ach'av said to `Ovadyah 1, Go through the land, to all the springs of water, and to all the brooks: peradventure we may find grass and save the horses and mules alive, that we not lose all the animals.

Brit Chadasha

2Corinthians 3:1-9

Are we beginning again to commend ourselves? Or do we need, as do some, letters of commendation to you or from you?

You are our letter, written in our hearts, known and read by all men; being revealed that you are a letter of Messiah, served by us, written not with ink, but with the Spirit of the living God; not in tablets of stone, but in tablets that are hearts of flesh.

Such confidence we have through Messiah toward God; not that we are sufficient of ourselves, to account anything as from ourselves; but our sufficiency is from God; who also made us sufficient as servants of a new covenant; not of the letter, but of the Spirit.

For the letter kills, but the Spirit gives life.

But if the service of death, written engraved on stones, came with glory, so that the children of Yisra'el could not look steadfastly on the face of Moshe for the glory of his face; which was passing away: won't service of the Spirit be with much more glory?

Parashat: Ki Tisa - "When You Elevate"

Daily Portion: Monday

Exodus 30:34-31:17

The LORD said to Moshe, "Take to yourself sweet spices, gum resin, and onycha, and galbanum; sweet spices with pure frankincense: of each shall there be an equal weight; and you shall make incense of it, a perfume after the art of the perfumer, seasoned with salt, pure and holy: and you shall beat some of it very small, and put some of it before the testimony in the tent of meeting, where I will meet with you. It shall be to you most holy. The incense which you shall make, according to its composition you shall not make for yourselves: it shall be to you holy for the LORD. Whoever shall make any like that, to smell of it, he shall be cut off from his people." The LORD spoke to Moshe, saying, "Behold, I have called by name Betzal'el the son of Uri, the son of Chur, of the tribe of Yehudah: and I have filled him with the Spirit of God, in wisdom, and in understanding, and in knowledge, and in all manner of workmanship, to devise skillful works, to work in gold, and in silver, and in brass, and in cutting of stones for setting, and in carving of wood, to work in all manner of workmanship. I, behold, I have appointed with him Oholi'av, the son of Achisamakh, of the tribe of Dan; and in the heart of all who are wise-hearted I have put wisdom, that they may make all that I have commanded you: the tent of meeting, the ark of the testimony, the mercy seat that is on it, all the furniture of the Tent, the table and its vessels, the pure menorah with all its vessels, the altar of incense, the altar of burnt offering with all its vessels, the basin and its base, the finely worked garments—the holy garments for Aharon the Kohen—the garments of his sons to minister in the Kohen's office, the anointing oil, and the incense of sweet spices for the holy place: according to all that I have commanded you they shall do."

The LORD spoke to Moshe, saying, "Speak also to the children of Yisra'el, saying, 'Most certainly you shall keep my Shabbatot: for it is a sign between Me and you throughout your generations; that you may know that I am the LORD who sanctifies you. You shall keep the Shabbat therefore; for it is holy to you. Everyone who profanes it shall surely be put to death; for whoever does any work therein, that soul shall be cut off from among his people. Six days shall work be done, but on the seventh day is a Shabbat of solemn rest, holy to the LORD. Whoever does any work on the day of Shabbat shall surely be put to death. Therefore the children of Yisra'el shall keep the Shabbat, to observe the Shabbat throughout their generations, for a perpetual covenant. It is a sign between Me and the children of Yisra'el forever; for in six days the LORD made heaven and earth, and on the seventh day He rested, and was refreshed.'"

Haftarah

1Kings 18:6-10

Parashat Ki Tisa — Day 2

So they divided the land between them to pass throughout it: Ach'av went one way by himself, and `Ovadyah 1 went another way by himself.

As `Ovadyah 1 was in the way, behold, Eliyahu met him: and he knew him, and fell on his face, and said, Is it you, my lord Eliyahu?

He answered him, It is I: go, tell your lord, Behold, Eliyahu [is here].

He said, Wherein have I sinned, that you would deliver your servant into the hand of Ach'av, to kill me?

As the LORD your God lives, there is no nation or kingdom, where my lord has not sent to seek you: and when they said, He is not here, he took an oath of the kingdom and nation, that they didn't find you.

Brit Chadasha

2Corinthians 3:10-18

For most certainly that which has been made glorious has not been made glorious in this respect, by reason of the glory that surpasses.

For if that which passes away was with glory, much more that which remains is in glory.

Having therefore such a hope, we use great boldness of speech, and not as Moshe, who put a veil on his face, that the children of Yisra'el wouldn't look steadfastly on the end of that which was passing away.

But their minds were hardened, for until this very day at the reading of the old covenant the same veil remains, because in Messiah it passes away.

But to this day, when Moshe is read, a veil lies on their heart. But whenever one turns to the Lord, the veil is taken away.

Now the Lord is the Spirit and where the Spirit of the Lord is, there is liberty. But we all, with unveiled face beholding as in a mirror the glory of the Lord, are transformed into the same image from glory to glory, even as from the Lord, the Spirit.

Parashat: Ki Tisa - "When You Elevate"

Daily Portion: Tuesday

Exodus 31:18-32:16

He gave to Moshe, when He finished speaking with him on Mount Sinai, the two tablets of the testimony, stone tablets, written with God's finger. When the people saw that Moshe delayed to come down from the mountain, the people gathered themselves together to Aharon, and said to him, "Come, make us gods, which shall go before us; for as for this Moshe, the man who brought us up out of the land of Egypt, we don't know what has become of him." Aharon said to them, "Take off the golden rings, which are in the ears of your wives, of your sons, and of your daughters, and bring them to me." All the people took off the golden rings which were in their ears, and brought them to Aharon. He received what they handed him, and fashioned it with an engraving tool, and made it a molten calf; and they said, "These are your gods, Yisra'el, which brought you up out of the land of Egypt." When Aharon saw this, he built an altar before it; and Aharon made a proclamation, and said, "Tomorrow shall be a feast to the LORD." They rose up early on the next day, and offered burnt offerings, and brought shalom offerings; and the people sat down to eat and to drink, and rose up to play. The LORD spoke to Moshe, "Go, get down; for your people, who you brought up out of the land of Egypt, have corrupted themselves! They have turned aside quickly out of the way which I commanded them. They have made themselves a molten calf, and have worshiped it, and have sacrificed to it, and said, 'These are your gods, Yisra'el, which brought you up out of the land of Egypt.'" The LORD said to Moshe, "I have seen these people, and behold, they are a stiff-necked people. Now therefore leave Me alone, that My wrath may burn hot against them, and that I may consume them; and I will make of you a great nation." Moshe begged the LORD his God, and said, "The LORD, why does Your wrath burn hot against Your people, that You have brought forth out of the land of Egypt with great power and with a mighty hand? Why should the Egyptians speak, saying, 'He brought them forth for evil, to kill them in the mountains, and to consume them from the surface of the earth?' Turn from Your fierce wrath, and repent of this evil against Your people. Remember Avraham, Yitzchak, and Yisra'el, Your servants, to whom You swore by Your own self, and said to them, 'I will multiply your seed as the stars of the sky, and all this land that I have spoken of I will give to your seed, and they shall inherit it forever.'" The LORD repented of the evil which He said He would do to His people. Moshe turned, and went down from the mountain, with the two tablets of the testimony in his hand; tablets that were written on both their sides; on the one side and on the other they were written. The tablets were the work of God, and the writing was the writing of God, engraved on the tables.

Haftarah

1Kings 18:11-16

Now you say, Go, tell your lord, Behold, Eliyahu [is here].

It will happen, as soon as I am gone from you, that the Spirit of the LORD will carry you I don't know where; and so when I come and tell Ach'av, and he can't find you, he will kill me: but I your servant fear the LORD from my youth.

Wasn't it told my lord what I did when Izevel killed the prophets of the LORD, how I hid one hundred men of the LORD's prophets by fifty in a cave, and fed them with bread and water?

Now you say, Go, tell your lord, Behold, Eliyahu [is here]; and he will kill me. Eliyahu said, As the LORD of Armies lives, before whom I stand, I will surely show myself to him today. So `Ovadyah 1 went to meet Ach'av, and told him; and Ach'av went to meet Eliyahu.

Brit Chadasha

1Corinthians 8:4-13

Therefore concerning the eating of things sacrificed to idols, we know that no idol is anything in the world, and that there is no other God but one.

For though there are things that are called "gods," whether in the heavens or on earth; as there are many "gods" and many "lords;" yet to us there is one God, the Father, of whom are all things, and we for Him; and one Lord, Yeshua the Messiah, through whom are all things, and we live through Him.

However, that knowledge isn't in all men. But some, with consciousness of the idol until now, eat as of a thing sacrificed to an idol, and their conscience, being weak, is defiled. But food will not commend us to God. For neither, if we don't eat, are we the worse; nor, if we eat, are we the better. But be careful that by no means does this liberty of yours become a stumbling block to the weak.

For if a man sees you who have knowledge sitting in an idol's temple, won't his conscience, if he is weak, be emboldened to eat things sacrificed to idols? And through your knowledge, he who is weak perishes, the brother for whose sake Messiah died. Thus, sinning against the brothers, and wounding their conscience when it is weak, you sin against Messiah.

Therefore, If food causes my brother to stumble, I will eat no meat forevermore, that I don't cause my brother to stumble.

Parashat Ki Tisa — Day 3

Parashat: Ki Tisa - "When You Elevate"
Daily Portion: Wednesday
Exodus 32:17-35

When Yehoshua heard the noise of the people as they shouted, he said to Moshe, "There is the noise of war in the camp." He said, "It isn't the voice of those who shout for victory, neither is it the voice of those who cry for being overcome; but the noise of those who sing that I hear." It happened, as soon as he came near to the camp, that he saw the calf and the dancing: and Moshe' anger grew hot, and he threw the tablets out of his hands, and broke them beneath the mountain. He took the calf which they had made, and burnt it with fire, ground it to powder, and scattered it on the water, and made the children of Yisra'el drink of it. Moshe said to Aharon, "What did these people do to you, that you have brought a great sin on them?" Aharon said, "Don't let the anger of my lord grow hot. You know the people, that they are set on evil. For they said to me, 'Make us gods, which shall go before us; for as for this Moshe, the man who brought us up out of the land of Egypt, we don't know what has become of him.' I said to them, 'Whoever has any gold, let them take it off:' so they gave it to me; and I threw it into the fire, and out came this calf."

When Moshe saw that the people had broken loose, (for Aharon had let them loose for a derision among their enemies), then Moshe stood in the gate of the camp, and said, "Whoever is on the LORD's side, come to me!" All the sons of Levi gathered themselves together to him. He said to them, "Thus says the LORD, the God of Yisra'el, 'Every man put his sword on his thigh, and go back and forth from gate to gate throughout the camp, and every man kill his brother, and every man his companion, and every man his neighbor.'" The sons of Levi did according to the word of Moshe: and there fell of the people that day about three thousand men. Moshe said, "Consecrate yourselves today to the LORD, yes, every man against his son, and against his brother; that he may bestow on you a blessing this day." It happened on the next day, that Moshe said to the people, "You have sinned a great sin. Now I will go up to the LORD. Perhaps I shall make atonement for your sin." Moshe returned to the LORD, and said, "Oh, this people have sinned a great sin, and have made themselves gods of gold. Yet now, if you will, forgive their sin—and if not, please blot me out of your book which you have written." The LORD said to Moshe, "Whoever has sinned against Me, him will I blot out of My book. Now go, lead the people to the place of which I have spoken to you. Behold, My angel shall go before you. Nevertheless in the day when I punish, I will punish them for their sin." The LORD struck the people, because they made the calf, which Aharon made.

Haftarah

1Kings 18:17-21

Parashat Ki Tisa
Day 4

It happened, when Ach'av saw Eliyahu, that Ach'av said to him, Is it you, you troubler of Yisra'el?

He answered, I have not troubled Yisra'el; but you, and your father's house, in that you have forsaken the mitzvot of the LORD, and you have followed the Ba`alim.

Now therefore send, and gather to me all Yisra'el to Mount Karmel, and the prophets of Ba`al four hundred fifty, and the prophets of the Asherah four hundred, who eat at Izevel's table.

So Ach'av sent to all the children of Yisra'el, and gathered the prophets together to Mount Karmel.

Eliyahu came near to all the people, and said, "How long will you waver between the two sides? If the LORD is God, follow him; but if Ba`al, then follow him." The people answered him not a word.

Brit Chadasha

Acts 7:35-43

"This Moshe, whom they refused, saying, 'Who made you a ruler and a judge?'— God has sent him as both a ruler and a deliverer by the hand of the angel who appeared to him in the bush. This man led them out, having worked wonders and signs in Egypt, in the Sea of Suf, and in the wilderness for forty years. This is that Moshe, who said to the children of Yisra'el, 'The Lord our God will raise up a prophet for you from among your brothers, like me.' This is he who was in the assembly in the wilderness with the angel that spoke to him on Mount Sinai, and with our fathers, who received living oracles to give to us, to whom our fathers wouldn't be obedient, but rejected him, and turned back in their hearts to Egypt, saying to Aharon, 'Make us gods that will go before us, for as for this Moshe, who led us out of the land of Egypt, we don't know what has become of him.' They made a calf in those days, and brought a sacrifice to the idol, and rejoiced in the works of their hands. But God turned, and gave them up to serve the army of the sky, as it is written in the book of the prophets, 'Did you offer to me slain animals and sacrifices forty years in the wilderness, O house of Yisra'el? You took up the tent of Molekh, the star of your god Reifan, the figures which you made to worship. I will carry you away beyond Bavel.'

Parashat: Ki Tisa - "When You Elevate"

Daily Portion: Thursday

Exodus 33:1-20

The LORD spoke to Moshe, "Depart, go up from here, you and the people that you have brought up out of the land of Egypt, to the land of which I swore to Avraham, to Yitzchak, and to Ya`akov, saying, 'I will give it to your seed.' I will send an angel before you; and I will drive out the Kena'ani, the Amori, and the Chittite, and the Perizzi, the Chivvi, and the Yevusi: to a land flowing with milk and honey: for I will not go up in the midst of you, for you are a stiff-necked people, lest I consume you in the way." When the people heard this evil news, they mourned: and no one put on his jewelry. The LORD said to Moshe, "Tell the children of Yisra'el, 'You are a stiff-necked people. If I were to go up into your midst for one moment, I would consume you. Therefore now take off your jewelry from you, that I may know what to do to you.'" The children of Yisra'el stripped themselves of their jewelry from Mount Chorev onward. Now Moshe used to take the tent and to pitch it outside the camp, far away from the camp, and he called it "The tent of meeting." It happened that everyone who sought the LORD went out to the tent of meeting, which was outside the camp. It happened that when Moshe went out to the Tent, that all the people rose up, and stood, everyone at their tent door, and watched Moshe, until he had gone into the Tent. It happened, when Moshe entered into the Tent, that the pillar of cloud descended, stood at the door of the Tent, and spoke with Moshe. All the people saw the pillar of cloud stand at the door of the Tent, and all the people rose up and worshiped, everyone at their tent door. The LORD spoke to Moshe face to face, as a man speaks to his friend. He turned again into the camp, but his servant Yehoshua, the son of Nun, a young man, didn't depart out of the Tent. Moshe said to the LORD, "Behold, you tell me, 'Bring up this people:' and you haven't let me know whom You will send with me. Yet You have said, 'I know you by name,' and you have also found favor in My sight.' Now therefore, if I have found favor in Your sight, please show me now Your ways, that I may know You, so that I may find favor in Your sight: and consider that this nation is Your people." He said, "My presence will go with you, and I will give you rest." He said to him, "If Your presence doesn't go with me, don't carry us up from here. For how would people know that I have found favor in Your sight, I and Your people? Isn't it in that You go with us, so that we are separated, I and Your people, from all the people who are on the surface of the earth?" The LORD said to Moshe, "I will do this thing also that you have spoken; for you have found favor in My sight, and I know you by name." He said, "Please show me Your glory." He said, "I will make all My goodness pass before you, and will proclaim the name of the LORD before you. I will be gracious to whom I will be gracious, and will show mercy on whom I will show mercy." He said, "You cannot see My face, for man may not see Me and live."

Haftarah

1Kings 18:22-26

Then Eliyahu said to the people, "I, even I only, am left a prophet of the LORD; but Ba`al's prophets are four hundred fifty men. Let them therefore give us two bulls; and let them choose one bull for themselves, and cut it in pieces, and lay it on the wood, and put no fire under; and I will dress the other bull, and lay it on the wood, and put no fire under. You call on the name of your god, and I will call on the name of the LORD; and the God who answers by fire, let him be God." All the people answered, "It is well said." Eliyahu said to the prophets of Ba`al, "Choose one bull for yourselves, and dress it first; for you are many; and call on the name of your god, but put no fire under it." They took the bull which was given them, and they dressed it, and called on the name of Ba`al from morning even until noon, saying, Ba`al, hear us. But there was no voice, nor any who answered. They leaped about the altar which was made.

Parashat Ki Tisa

Day 5

Brit Chadasha

Acts 7:44-8:1

"Our fathers had the tent of the testimony in the wilderness, even as He who spoke to Moshe commanded him to make it according to the pattern that he had seen; which also our fathers, in their turn, brought in with Yehoshua when they entered into the possession of the nations, whom God drove out before the face of our fathers, to the days of David, who found favor in the sight of God, and asked to find a habitation for the God of Ya`akov. But Shlomo built Him a house. However, the Elyon doesn't dwell in temples made with hands, as the prophet says, 'heaven is My throne, and the earth a footstool for My feet. What kind of house will you build Me?' says the Lord; 'or what is the place of My rest? Didn't My hand make all these things?' "You stiff-necked and uncircumcised in heart and ears, you always resist the Holy Spirit! As your fathers did, so you do. Which of the prophets didn't your fathers persecute? They killed those who foretold the coming of the Righteous One, of whom you have now become betrayers and murderers. You received the Torah as it was ordained by angels, and didn't keep it!" Now when they heard these things, they were cut to the heart, and they gnashed at him with their teeth. But he, being full of the Holy Spirit, looked up steadfastly into heaven, and saw the glory of God, and Yeshua standing on the right hand of God, and said, "Behold, I see the heavens opened, and the Son of Man standing at the right hand of God!" But they cried out with a loud voice, and stopped their ears, and rushed at him with one accord. They threw him out of the city, and stoned him. The witnesses placed their garments at the feet of a young man named Sha'ul. They stoned Stephen as he called out, saying, "Lord Yeshua, receive my Spirit!" He kneeled down, and cried with a loud voice, "Lord, don't hold this sin against them!" When he had said this, he fell asleep. Sha'ul was consenting to his death. A great persecution arose against the assembly which was in Yerushalayim in that day. They were all scattered abroad throughout the regions of Yehudah and Shomron, except for the emissaries.

Parashat: Ki Tisa - "When You Elevate"

Daily Portion: Friday

Exodus 33:21-34:17

The LORD also said, "Behold, there is a place by Me, and you shall stand on the rock. It will happen, while My glory passes by, that I will put you in a cleft of the rock, and will cover you with My hand until I have passed by; then I will take away My hand, and you will see My back; but My face shall not be seen." The LORD said to Moshe, "Chisel two stone tablets like the first: and I will write on the tablets the words that were on the first tablets, which you broke. Be ready by the morning, and come up in the morning to Mount Sinai, and present yourself there to Me on the top of the mountain. No one shall come up with you; neither let anyone be seen throughout all the mountain; neither let the flocks nor herds feed before that mountain." He chiseled two tablets of stone like the first; and Moshe rose up early in the morning, and went up to Mount Sinai, as the LORD had commanded him, and took in his hand two stone tablets. The LORD descended in the cloud, and stood with him there, and proclaimed the name of the LORD. The LORD passed by before him, and proclaimed, "The LORD! the LORD, a merciful and gracious God, slow to anger, and abundant in loving kindness and truth, keeping loving kindness for thousands, forgiving iniquity and disobedience and sin; and that will by no means clear the guilty, visiting the iniquity of the fathers on the children, and on the children's children, on the third and on the fourth generation." Moshe hurried and bowed his head toward the earth, and worshiped. He said, "If now I have found favor in your sight, Lord, please let the Lord go in the midst of us; although this is a stiff-necked people; pardon our iniquity and our sin, and take us for Your inheritance." He said, "Behold, I make a covenant: before all your people I will do marvels, such as have not been worked in all the earth, nor in any nation; and all the people among which you are shall see the work of the LORD; for it is an awesome thing that I do with you. Observe that which I command you this day. Behold, I drive out before you the Amori, the Kena'ani, the Chittite, the Perizzi, the Chivvi, and the Yevusi. Be careful, lest you make a covenant with the inhabitants of the land where you are going, lest it be for a snare in the midst of you: but you shall break down their altars, and dash in pieces their pillars, and you shall cut down their Asherim; for you shall worship no other god: for the LORD, whose name is Jealous, is a jealous God. Don't make a covenant with the inhabitants of the land, lest they play the prostitute after their gods, and sacrifice to their gods, and one call you and you eat of his sacrifice; and you take of their daughters to your sons, and their daughters play the prostitute after their gods, and make your sons play the prostitute after their gods. You shall make no cast idols for yourselves.

Haftarah

1 Kings 18:27-32

Parashat Ki Tisa
Day 6

It happened at noon, that Eliyahu mocked them, and said, Cry aloud; for he is a god: either he is musing, or he is gone aside, or he is on a journey, or peradventure he sleeps and must be awakened.

They cried aloud, and cut themselves after their manner with knives and lances, until the blood gushed out on them.

It was so, when midday was past, that they prophesied until the time of the offering of the [evening] offering; but there was neither voice, nor any to answer, nor any who regarded.

Eliyahu said to all the people, Come near to me; and all the people came near to him. He repaired the altar of the LORD that was thrown down.

Eliyahu took twelve stones, according to the number of the tribes of the sons of Ya`akov, to whom the word of the LORD came, saying, Yisra'el shall be your name.

With the stones he built an altar in the name of the LORD; and he made a trench about the altar, as great as would contain two measures of seed.

Brit Chadasha

Luke 11:14-20

He was casting out a demon, and it was mute. It happened, when the demon had gone out, the mute man spoke; and the multitudes marveled. But some of them said, "He casts out demons by Ba`al-Zibbul, the prince of the demons." Others, testing Him, sought from Him a sign from heaven.

But He, knowing their thoughts, said to them, "Every kingdom divided against itself Is brought to desolation. A house divided against itself falls. If Hasatan also is divided against himself, how will his kingdom stand? For you say that I cast out demons by Ba`al-Zibbul.

But if I cast out demons by Ba`al-Zibbul, by whom do your children cast them out? Therefore will they be your judges. But if I by the finger of God cast out demons, then the Kingdom of God has come to you.

Parashat: Ki Tisa - "When You Elevate"

Daily Portion: Shabbat

Exodus 34:18-35

"You shall keep the feast of matzah. Seven days you shall eat matzah, as I commanded you, at the time appointed in the month Aviv; for in the month Aviv you came out from Egypt. All that opens the womb is Mine; and all your livestock that is male, the firstborn of cow and sheep. The firstborn of a donkey you shall redeem with a lamb: and if you will not redeem it, then you shall break its neck. All the firstborn of your sons you shall redeem. No one shall appear before Me empty. "Six days you shall work, but on the seventh day you shall rest: in plowing time and in harvest you shall rest. You shall observe the feast of weeks with the first fruits of wheat harvest, and the Chag-HaKatzir at the year's end. Three times in the year all your males shall appear before the Lord GOD, the God of Yisra'el. For I will drive out nations before you and enlarge your borders; neither shall any man desire your land when you go up to appear before the LORD, your God, three times in the year. "You shall not offer the blood of My sacrifice with leavened bread; neither shall the sacrifice of the feast of the Pesach be left to the morning. You shall bring the first of the first fruits of your ground to the house of the LORD your God. You shall not boil a young goat in its mother's milk."

The LORD said to Moshe, "Write you these words: for in accordance with these words I have made a covenant with you and with Yisra'el." He was there with the LORD forty days and forty nights; he neither ate bread, nor drank water. He wrote on the tablets the words of the covenant, the ten mitzvot. It happened, when Moshe came down from Mount Sinai with the two tablets of the testimony in Moshe' hand, when he came down from the mountain, that Moshe didn't know that the skin of his face shone by reason of his speaking with Him. When Aharon and all the children of Yisra'el saw Moshe, behold, the skin of his face shone; and they were afraid to come near him. Moshe called to them, and Aharon and all the rulers of the congregation returned to him; and Moshe spoke to them. Afterward all the children of Yisra'el came near, and he gave them all of the mitzvot that the LORD had spoken with him on Mount Sinai. When Moshe was done speaking with them, he put a veil on his face. But when Moshe went in before the LORD to speak with Him, he took the veil off, until he came out; and he came out, and spoke to the children of Yisra'el that which He was commanded. The children of Yisra'el saw Moshe' face, that the skin of Moshe' face shone: and Moshe put the veil on his face again, until he went in to speak with Him.

Haftarah

1Kings 18:33-39

He put the wood in order, and cut the bull in pieces, and laid it on the wood. He said, Fill four jars with water, and pour it on the burnt offering, and on the wood. He said, Do it the second time; and they did it the second time. He said, Do it the third time; and they did it the third time. The water ran round about the altar; and he filled the trench also with water.

It happened at the time of the offering of the [evening] offering, that Eliyahu the prophet came near, and said, LORD, the God of Avraham, of Yitzchak, and of Yisra'el, let it be known this day that you are God in Yisra'el, and that I am your servant, and that I have done all these things at your word.

Hear me, LORD, hear me, that this people may know that you, LORD, are God, and [that] you have turned their heart back again. Then the fire of the LORD fell, and consumed the burnt offering, and the wood, and the stones, and the dust, and licked up the water that was in the trench. When all the people saw it, they fell on their faces, and they said, the LORD, he is God; the LORD, he is God.

Brit Chadasha

1Corinthians 10:1-13

Now I would not have you ignorant, brothers, that our fathers were all under the cloud, and all passed through the sea; and were all immersed into Moshe in the cloud and in the sea; and all ate the same spiritual food; and all drank the same spiritual drink. For they drank of a spiritual rock that followed them, and the rock was Messiah. However with most of them, God was not well pleased, for they were overthrown in the wilderness. Now these things were our examples, to the intent we should not lust after evil things, as they also lusted. Neither be idolaters, as some of them were. As it is written, "The people sat down to eat and drink, and rose up to play." Neither let us commit sexual immorality, as some of them committed, and in one day twenty-three thousand fell. Neither let us test the Lord, as some of them tested, and perished by the serpents. Neither grumble, as some of them also grumbled, and perished by the destroyer. Now all these things happened to them by way of example, and they were written for our admonition, on whom the ends of the ages have come. Therefore let him who thinks he stands be careful that he doesn't fall. No temptation has taken you except what is common to man. God is faithful, who will not allow you to be tempted above what you are able, but will with the temptation also make the way of escape, that you may be able to endure it.

> Parashat Ki Tisa
> Day 7

Parashat: Vayakhel - "And He Assembled"

Daily Portion: Sunday

Exodus 35:1-19

Moshe assembled all the congregation of the children of Yisra'el, and said to them, "These are the words which the LORD has commanded, that you should do them.

'Six days shall work be done, but on the seventh day there shall be a holy day for you, a Shabbat of solemn rest to the LORD: whoever does any work in it shall be put to death.

You shall kindle no fire throughout your habitations on the day of Shabbat.'"

Moshe spoke to all the congregation of the children of Yisra'el, saying, "This is the thing which the LORD commanded, saying, 'Take from among you an offering to the LORD.

Whoever is of a willing heart, let him bring it, the LORD's offering: gold, silver, brass, blue, purple, scarlet, fine linen, goats' hair, rams' skins dyed red, sea cow hides, shittim wood, oil for the light, spices for the anointing oil and for the sweet incense, shoham stones, and stones to be set for the efod and for the breastplate."

'Let every wise-hearted man among you come, and make all that the LORD has commanded: the tent, its outer covering, its roof, its clasps, its boards, its bars, its pillars, and its sockets; the ark, and its poles, the mercy seat, the veil of the screen; the table with its poles and all its vessels, and the show bread; the menorah also for the light, with its vessels, its lamps, and the oil for the light; and the altar of incense with its poles, the anointing oil, the sweet incense, the screen for the door, at the door of the tent; the altar of burnt offering, with its grating of brass, it poles, and all its vessels, the basin and its base; the hangings of the court, its pillars, their sockets, and the screen for the gate of the court; the pins of the tent, the pins of the court, and their cords; the finely worked garments, for ministering in the holy place, the holy garments for Aharon the Kohen, and the garments of his sons, to minister in the Kohen's office.'"

Haftarah

1Kings 7:13-17

King Shlomo sent and fetched Chiram out of Tzor. He was the son of a widow of the tribe of Naftali, and his father was a man of Tzor, a worker in brass; and he was filled with wisdom and understanding and skill, to work all works in brass. He came to king Shlomo, and performed all his work.

For he fashioned the two pillars of brass, eighteen cubits high apiece: and a line of twelve cubits compassed either of them about.

He made two capitals of molten brass, to set on the tops of the pillars: the height of the one capital was five cubits, and the height of the other capital was five cubits.

There were nets of checker work, and wreaths of chain work, for the capitals which were on the top of the pillars; seven for the one capital, and seven for the other capital.

Parashat Vayakhel

Day 1

Brit Chadasha

2Corinthians 8:1-15

Moreover, brothers, we make known to you the grace of God which has been given in the assemblies of Macedonia; how that in much proof of affliction the abundance of their joy and their deep poverty abounded to the riches of their liberality.

For according to their power, I testify, yes and beyond their power, they gave of their own accord, begging us with much entreaty to receive this grace and the fellowship in the service to the holy ones. This was not as we had hoped, but first they gave their own selves to the Lord, and to us through the will of God.

So we urged Titus, that as he made a beginning before, so he would also complete in you this grace. But as you abound in everything, in faith, utterance, knowledge, all earnestness, and in your love to us, see that you also abound in this grace.

I speak not by way of mitzvah, but as proving through the earnestness of others the sincerity also of your love.

For you know the grace of our Lord Yeshua the Messiah, that, though He was rich, yet for your sakes He became poor, that you through His poverty might become rich.

I give a judgment in this: for this is expedient for you, who were the first to start a year ago, not only to do, but also to be willing.

But now complete the doing also, that as there was the readiness to be willing, so there may be the completion also out of your ability. For if the readiness is there, it is acceptable according to what you have, not according to what you don't have.

For this is not that others may be eased and you distressed, but for equality. Your abundance at this present time supplies their lack, that their abundance also may become a supply for your lack; that there may be equality.

As it is written, "He who gathered much had nothing left over, and he who gathered little had no lack."

Parashat: Vayakhel - "And He Assembled"

Daily Portion: Monday

Exodus 35:20-35:34

All the congregation of the children of Yisra'el departed from the presence of Moshe.

They came, everyone whose heart stirred him up, and everyone whom his spirit made willing, and brought the LORD's offering, for the work of the tent of meeting, and for all of its service, and for the holy garments.

They came, both men and women, as many as were willing-hearted, and brought brooches, earrings, signet rings, and armlets, all jewels of gold; even every man who offered an offering of gold to the LORD.

Everyone, with whom was found blue, purple, scarlet, fine linen, goats' hair, rams' skins dyed red, and sea cow hides, brought them. Everyone who did offer an offering of silver and brass brought the LORD's offering; and everyone, with whom was found shittim wood for any work of the service, brought it.

All the women who were wise-hearted spun with their hands, and brought that which they had spun, the blue, the purple, the scarlet, and the fine linen.

All the women whose heart stirred them up in wisdom spun the goats' hair.

The rulers brought the shoham stones, and the stones to be set, for the efod and for the breastplate; and the spice, and the oil for the light, for the anointing oil, and for the sweet incense.

The children of Yisra'el brought a freewill offering to the LORD; every man and woman, whose heart made them willing to bring for all the work, which the LORD had commanded to be made by Moshe.

Moshe said to the children of Yisra'el, "Behold, the LORD has called by name Betzal'el the son of Uri, the son of Chur, of the tribe of Yehudah.

He has filled him with the Spirit of God, in wisdom, in understanding, in knowledge, and in all manner of workmanship; and to make skillful works, to work in gold, in silver, in brass, in cutting of stones for setting, and in carving of wood, to work in all kinds of skillful workmanship.

He has put in his heart that he may teach, both he, and Oholi'av, the son of Achisamakh, of the tribe of Dan.

Haftarah

1Kings 7:18-19

So he made the pillars; and there were two rows round about on the one network, to cover the capitals that were on the top of the pillars: and so did he for the other capital.

The capitals that were on the top of the pillars in the porch were of lily work, four cubits.

Parashat Vayakhel — Day 2

Brit Chadasha

2Corinthians 9:1-5

It is indeed unnecessary for me to write to you concerning the service to the holy ones, for I know your readiness, of which I boast on your behalf to them of Macedonia, that Achaia has been prepared for a year past.

Your zeal has stirred up very many of them.

But I have sent the brothers that our boasting on your behalf may not be in vain in this respect, that, just as I said, you may be prepared, so that I won't by any means, if there come with me any of Macedonia and find you unprepared, we (to say nothing of you) should be disappointed in this confident boasting.

I thought it necessary therefore to entreat the brothers that they would go before to you, and arrange ahead of time the generous gift that you promised before, that the same might be ready as a matter of generosity, and not of greediness.

Parashat: Vayakhel - "And He Assembled"

Daily Portion: Tuesday

Exodus 35:35-36:9

He has filled them with wisdom of heart, to work all manner of workmanship, of the engraver, of the skillful workman, and of the embroiderer, in blue, in purple, in scarlet, and in fine linen, and of the weaver, even of those who do any workmanship, and of those who make skillful works.

"Betzal'el and Oholi'av shall work with every wise-hearted man, in whom the LORD has put wisdom and understanding to know how to work all the work for the service of the sanctuary, according to all that the LORD has commanded."

Moshe called Betzal'el and Oholi'av, and every wise-hearted man, in whose heart the LORD had put wisdom, even everyone whose heart stirred him up to come to the work to do it: and they received from Moshe all the offering which the children of Yisra'el had brought for the work of the service of the sanctuary, with which to make it.

They brought yet to him freewill offerings every morning.

All the wise men, who performed all the work of the sanctuary, each came from his work which they did.

They spoke to Moshe, saying, "The people bring much more than enough for the service of the work which the LORD commanded to make."

Moshe gave mitzvah, and they caused it to be proclaimed throughout the camp, saying, "Let neither man nor woman make anything else for the offering for the sanctuary."

So the people were restrained from bringing.

For the stuff they had was sufficient for all the work to make it, and too much.

All the wise-hearted men among those who did the work made the tent with ten curtains; of fine twined linen, blue, purple, and scarlet, with Keruvim, the work of the skillful workman, they made them.

The length of each curtain was twenty-eight cubits, and the breadth of each curtain four cubits.

Haftarah

1Kings 7:20-21

Parashat Vayakhel

Day 3

There were capitals above also on the two pillars, close by the belly which was beside the network: and the pomegranates were two hundred, in rows round about on the other capital.

He set up the pillars at the porch of the temple: and he set up the right pillar, and called the name of it Yakhin; and he set up the left pillar, and called the name of it Bo`az.

Brit Chadasha

2Corinthians 9:6-15

Remember this: he who sows sparingly will also reap sparingly. He who sows bountifully will also reap bountifully.

Let each man give according as he has determined in his heart; not grudgingly, or under compulsion; for God loves a cheerful giver.

And God is able to make all grace abound to you, that you, always having all sufficiency in everything, may abound to every good work.

As it is written, "He has scattered abroad, He has given to the poor. His righteousness remains forever."

Now may He who supplies seed to the sower and bread for food, supply and multiply your seed for sowing, and increase the fruits of your righteousness; you being enriched in everything to all liberality, which works through us thanksgiving to God.

For this service of giving that you perform not only makes up for lack among the holy ones, but abounds also through many givings of thanks to God; seeing that through the proof given by this service, they glorify God for the obedience of your confession to the Good News of Messiah, and for the liberality of your contribution to them and to all; while they themselves also, with supplication on your behalf, yearn for you by reason of the exceeding grace of God in you.

Now thanks be to God for His unspeakable gift!

Parashat: Vayakhel - "And He Assembled"
Daily Portion: Wednesday
Exodus 36:10-36:26

All the curtains had one measure. He coupled five curtains to one another, and the other five curtains he coupled one to another.

He made loops of blue on the edge of the one curtain from the edge in the coupling. Likewise he made in the edge of the curtain that was outmost in the second coupling.

He made fifty loops in the one curtain, and he made fifty loops in the edge of the curtain that was in the second coupling. The loops were opposite one to another.

He made fifty clasps of gold, and coupled the curtains one to another with the clasps: so the tent was a unit.

He made curtains of goats' hair for a covering over the tent. He made them eleven curtains.

The length of each curtain was thirty cubits, and four cubits the breadth of each curtain. The eleven curtains had one measure.

He coupled five curtains by themselves, and six curtains by themselves.

He made fifty loops on the edge of the curtain that was outmost in the coupling, and he made fifty loops on the edge of the curtain which was outmost in the second coupling.

He made fifty clasps of brass to couple the tent together, that it might be a unit. He made a covering for the tent of rams' skins dyed red, and a covering of sea cow hides above.

He made the boards for the tent of shittim wood, standing up. Ten cubits was the length of a board, and a cubit and a half the breadth of each board. Each board had two tenons, joined one to another. He made all the boards of the tent this way.

He made the boards for the tent: twenty boards for the south side southward. He made forty sockets of silver under the twenty boards; two sockets under one board for its two tenons, and two sockets under another board for its two tenons.

For the second side of the tent, on the north side, he made twenty boards, and their forty sockets of silver; two sockets under one board, and two sockets under another board.

Haftarah
1 Kings 7:22-24

Parashat Vayakhel

Day 4

On the top of the pillars was lily work: so was the work of the pillars finished. He made the molten sea of ten cubits from brim to brim, round in compass, and the height of it was five cubits; and a line of thirty cubits compassed it round about.

Under the brim of it round about there were buds which did compass it, for ten cubits, compassing the sea round about: the buds were in two rows, cast when it was cast.

Brit Chadasha
1 Corinthians 2:6-10

We speak wisdom, however, among those who are full grown; yet a wisdom not of this world, nor of the rulers of this world, who are coming to nothing.

But we speak God's wisdom in a mystery, the wisdom that has been hidden, which God foreordained before the worlds for our glory, which none of the rulers of this world has known.

For had they known it, they wouldn't have crucified the Lord of glory.

But as it is written, "Things which an eye didn't see, and an ear didn't hear, which didn't enter into the heart of man, these God has prepared for those who love him."

But to us, God revealed them through the Spirit.

For the Spirit searches all things, yes, the deep things of God.

Parashat: Vayakhel - "And He Assembled"

Daily Portion: Thursday

Exodus 36:27-37:4

For the far part of the tent westward he made six boards. He made two boards for the corners of the tent in the far part.

They were double beneath, and in like manner they were all the way to the top of it to one ring. He did thus to both of them in the two corners.

There were eight boards, and their sockets of silver, sixteen sockets; under every board two sockets.

He made bars of shittim wood; five for the boards of the one side of the tent, and five bars for the boards of the other side of the tent, and five bars for the boards of the tent for the hinder part westward.

He made the middle bar to pass through in the midst of the boards from the one end to the other.

He overlaid the boards with gold, and made their rings of gold for places for the bars, and overlaid the bars with gold.

He made the veil of blue, purple, scarlet, and fine twined linen: with Keruvim. He made it the work of a skillful workman.

He made four pillars of shittim for it, and overlaid them with gold. Their hooks were of gold.

He cast four sockets of silver for them. He made a screen for the door of the tent, of blue, purple, scarlet, and fine twined linen, the work of an embroiderer; and the five pillars of it with their hooks.

He overlaid their capitals and their fillets with gold, and their five sockets were of brass.

Betzal'el made the ark of shittim wood. Its length was two and a half cubits, and its breadth a cubit and a half, and a cubit and a half its height.

He overlaid it with pure gold inside and outside, and made a molding of gold for it round about.

He cast four rings of gold for it, in its four feet; even two rings on its one side, and two rings on its other side. He made poles of shittim wood, and overlaid them with gold.

142 / The Daily Torah: Shemot

Haftarah

1 Kings 7:25-26

It stood on twelve oxen, three looking toward the north, and three looking toward the west, and three looking toward the south, and three looking toward the east; and the sea was set on them above, and all their hinder parts were inward.

It was a handbreadth thick: and the brim of it was worked like the brim of a cup, like the flower of a lily: it held two thousand baths.

Parashat Vayakhel

Day 5

Brit Chadasha

1 Corinthians 2:11-16

For who among men knows the things of a man, except the spirit of the man, which is in him?

Even so, no one knows the things of God, except God's Spirit.

But we received, not the spirit of the world, but the Spirit which is from God, that we might know the things that were freely given to us by God.

Which things also we speak, not in words which man's wisdom teaches, but which the Holy Spirit teaches, comparing spiritual things with spiritual things.

Now the natural man doesn't receive the things of God's Spirit, for they are foolishness to him, and he can't know them, because they are spiritually discerned.

But he who is spiritual discerns all things, and he himself is judged by no one.

"For who has known the mind of the Lord, that he should instruct Him?"

But we have Messiah's mind.

Parashat Vayakhel

Day 6

Parashat: Vayakhel - "And He Assembled"

Daily Portion: Friday

Exodus 37:5-27

He put the poles into the rings on the sides of the ark, to bear the ark. He made a mercy seat of pure gold. Its length was two and a half cubits, and a cubit and a half its breadth. He made two Keruvim of gold. He made them of beaten work, at the two ends of the mercy seat; one Keruv at the one end, and one Keruv at the other end. He made the Keruvim of one piece with the mercy seat at its two ends. The Keruvim spread out their wings on high, covering the mercy seat with their wings, with their faces toward one another.

The faces of the Keruvim were toward the mercy seat. He made the table of shittim wood. Its length was two cubits, and its breadth was a cubit, and its height was a cubit and a half. He overlaid it with pure gold, and made a gold molding around it. He made a border of a handbreadth around it, and made a golden molding on its border around it. He cast four rings of gold for it, and put the rings in the four corners that were on its four feet. The rings were close by the border, the places for the poles to carry the table. He made the poles of shittim wood, and overlaid them with gold, to carry the table. He made the vessels which were on the table, its dishes, its spoons, its bowls, and its pitchers with which to pour out, of pure gold.

He made the menorah of pure gold. He made the menorah of beaten work. Its base, its shaft, its cups, its buds, and its flowers were of one piece with it. There were six branches going out of its sides: three branches of the menorah out of its one side, and three branches of the menorah out of its other side: three cups made like almond blossoms in one branch, a bud and a flower, and three cups made like almond blossoms in the other branch, a bud and a flower: so for the six branches going out of the menorah.

In the menorah were four cups made like almond blossoms, its buds and its flowers; and a bud under two branches of one piece with it, and a bud under two branches of one piece with it, and a bud under two branches of one piece with it, for the six branches going out of it. Their buds and their branches were of one piece with it. The whole thing was one beaten work of pure gold. He made its seven lamps, and its snuffers, and its snuff dishes, of pure gold. He made it of a talent of pure gold, with all its vessels.

He made the altar of incense of shittim wood. It was square: its length was a cubit, and its breadth a cubit. Its height was two cubits. Its horns were of one piece with it. He overlaid it with pure gold, its top, its sides around it, and its horns. He made a gold molding around it. He made two golden rings for it under its molding crown, on its two ribs, on its two sides, for places for poles with which to carry it.

Haftarah

1Kings 7:40-45

Chiram made the basins, and the shovels, and the basins. So Chiram made an end of doing all the work that he worked for king Shlomo in the house of the LORD: the two pillars, and the two bowls of the capitals that were on the top of the pillars; and the two networks to cover the two bowls of the capitals that were on the top of the pillars; and the four hundred pomegranates for the two networks; two rows of pomegranates for each network, to cover the two bowls of the capitals that were on the pillars; and the ten bases, and the ten basins on the bases; and the one sea, and the twelve oxen under the sea; and the pots, and the shovels, and the basins: even all these vessels, which Chiram made for king Shlomo, in the house of the LORD, were of burnished brass.

Parashat Vayakhel — Day 6

Brit Chadasha

1Corinthians 3:1-9

Brothers, I couldn't speak to you as to spiritual, but as to fleshly, as to babies in Messiah.

I fed you with milk, not with meat; for you weren't yet ready.

Indeed, not even now are you ready, for you are still fleshly.

For insofar as there is jealousy, strife, and factions among you, aren't you fleshly, and don't you walk in the ways of men?

For when one says, "I follow Sha'ul," and another, "I follow Apollos," aren't you fleshly?

Who then is Apollos, and who is Sha'ul, but servants through whom you believed; and each as the Lord gave to him?

I planted. Apollos watered. But God gave the increase.

So then neither he who plants is anything, nor he who waters, but God who gives the increase.

Now he who plants and he who waters are the same, but each will receive his own reward according to his own labor.

For we are God's fellow workers. You are God's farming, God's building.

Parashat: Vayakhel - "And He Assembled"

Daily Portion: Shabbat

Exodus 37:28-38:20

He made the poles of shittim wood, and overlaid them with gold. He made the holy anointing oil and the pure incense of sweet spices, after the art of the perfumer. He made the altar of burnt offering of shittim wood. It was square. Its length was five cubits, its breadth was five cubits, and its height was three cubits. He made its horns on its four corners. Its horns were of one piece with it, and he overlaid it with brass.

He made all the vessels of the altar, the pots, the shovels, the basins, the forks, and the fire pans. He made all its vessels of brass. He made for the altar a grating of a network of brass, under the ledge around it beneath, reaching halfway up. He cast four rings for the four ends of brass grating, to be places for the poles.

He made the poles of shittim wood, and overlaid them with brass. He put the poles into the rings on the sides of the altar, with which to carry it. He made it hollow with planks.

He made the basin of brass, and its base of brass, out of the mirrors of the ministering women who ministered at the door of the tent of meeting. He made the court: for the south side southward the hangings of the court were of fine twined linen, one hundred cubits; their pillars were twenty, and their sockets twenty, of brass; the hooks of the pillars and their fillets were of silver. For the north side one hundred cubits, their pillars twenty, and their sockets twenty, of brass; the hooks of the pillars, and their fillets, of silver.

For the west side were hangings of fifty cubits, their pillars ten, and their sockets ten; the hooks of the pillars, and their fillets, of silver. For the east side eastward fifty cubits. The hangings for the one side were fifteen cubits; their pillars three, and their sockets three; and so for the other side: on this hand and that hand by the gate of the court were hangings of fifteen cubits; their pillars three, and their sockets three.

All the hangings around the court were of fine twined linen. The sockets for the pillars were of brass. The hooks of the pillars and their fillets were of silver; and the overlaying of their capitals, of silver; and all the pillars of the court were filleted with silver. The screen for the gate of the court was the work of the embroiderer, of blue, purple, scarlet, and fine twined linen.

Twenty cubits was the length, and the height in the breadth was five cubits, like to the hangings of the court. Their pillars were four, and their sockets four, of brass; their hooks of silver, and the overlaying of their capitals, and their fillets, of silver. All the pins of the tent, and around the court, were of brass.

Haftarah

1 Kings 7:46-50

In the plain of the Yarden did the king cast them, in the clay ground between Sukkot and Tzaretan.

Shlomo left all the vessels [unweighed], because they were exceeding many: the weight of the brass could not be found out. Shlomo made all the vessels that were in the house of the LORD: the golden altar, and the table whereupon the show bread was, of gold; and the menorot, five on the right side, and five on the left, before the oracle, of pure gold; and the flowers, and the lamps, and the tongs, of gold; and the cups, and the snuffers, and the basins, and the spoons, and the fire pans, of pure gold; and the hinges, both for the doors of the inner house, the most holy place, and for the doors of the house, [to wit], of the temple, of gold.

Parashat Vayakhel — Day 7

Brit Chadasha

1 Corinthians 3:10-17

According to the grace of God which was given to me, as a wise master builder I laid a foundation, and another builds on it.

But let each man be careful how he builds on it. For no one can lay any other foundation than that which has been laid, which is Yeshua the Messiah.

But if anyone builds on the foundation with gold, silver, costly stones, wood, hay, or stubble; each man's work will be revealed.

For the Day will declare it, because it is revealed in fire; and the fire itself will test what sort of work each man's work is.

If any man's work remains which he built on it, he will receive a reward. If any man's work is burned, he will suffer loss, but he himself will be saved, but as through fire.

Don't you know that you are a temple of God, and that God's Spirit lives in you?

If anyone destroys the temple of God, God will destroy him; for God's temple is holy, which you are.

Parashat: Pekudei - "Accounts Of"

Daily Portion: Sunday

Exodus 38:21-38:28

This is the amount of material used for the tent, even the Tent of the Testimony, as they were counted, according to the mitzvah of Moshe, for the service of the Levites, by the hand of Itamar, the son of Aharon the Kohen.

Betzal'el the son of Uri, the son of Chur, of the tribe of Yehudah, made all that the LORD commanded Moshe.

With him was Oholi'av, the son of Achisamakh, of the tribe of Dan, an engraver, and a skillful workman, and an embroiderer in blue, in purple, in scarlet, and in fine linen.

All the gold that was used for the work in all the work of the sanctuary, even the gold of the offering, was twenty-nine talents, and seven hundred thirty shekels, after the shekel of the sanctuary.

The silver of those who were numbered of the congregation was one hundred talents, and one thousand seven hundred seventy-five shekels, after the shekel of the sanctuary: a beka a head, that is, half a shekel, after the shekel of the sanctuary, for everyone who passed over to those who were numbered, from twenty years old and upward, for six hundred three thousand five hundred fifty men.

The one hundred talents of silver were for casting the sockets of the sanctuary, and the sockets of the veil; one hundred sockets for the one hundred talents, a talent for a socket.

Of the one thousand seven hundred seventy-five shekels he made hooks for the pillars, overlaid their capitals, and made fillets for them.

Haftarah

1Kings 7:51-8:5

Thus all the work that king Shlomo worked in the house of the LORD was finished. Shlomo brought in the things which David his father had dedicated, [even] the silver, and the gold, and the vessels, and put them in the treasuries of the house of the LORD.

> **Parashat Pekudei**
> **Day 1**

Then Shlomo assembled the elders of Yisra'el, and all the heads of the tribes, the princes of the fathers' [houses] of the children of Yisra'el, to king Shlomo in Yerushalayim, to bring up the ark of the covenant of the LORD out of the city of David, which is Tziyon.

All the men of Yisra'el assembled themselves to king Shlomo at the feast, in the month Etanim, which is the seventh month.

All the elders of Yisra'el came, and the Kohanim took up the ark.

They brought up the ark of the LORD, and the tent of meeting, and all the holy vessels that were in the Tent; even these did the Kohanim and the Levites bring up.

King Shlomo and all the congregation of Yisra'el, who were assembled to him, were with him before the ark, sacrificing sheep and oxen, that could not be counted nor numbered for multitude.

Brit Chadasha
Hebrews 9:1-7

Now indeed even the first covenant had ordinances of divine service, and an earthly sanctuary.

For a tabernacle was prepared. In the first part were the menorah, the table, and the show bread; which is called the Holy Place.

After the second veil was the tabernacle which is called the Holy of Holies, having a golden altar of incense, and the ark of the covenant overlaid on all sides with gold, in which was a golden pot holding the manna, Aharon's rod that budded, and the tablets of the covenant; and above it Keruvim of glory overshadowing the mercy seat, of which things we can't speak now in detail.

Now these things having been thus prepared, the Kohanim go in continually into the first tabernacle, accomplishing the services, but into the second the Kohen Gadol alone, once in the year, not without blood, which he offers for himself, and for the errors of the people.

Parashat: Pekudei - "Accounts Of"

Daily Portion: Monday

Exodus 38:29-39:13

The brass of the offering was seventy talents, and two thousand four hundred shekels.

With this he made the sockets to the door of the tent of meeting, the bronze altar, the bronze grating for it, all the vessels of the altar, the sockets around the court, the sockets of the gate of the court, all the pins of the tent, and all the pins around the court.

Of the blue, purple, and scarlet, they made finely worked garments, for ministering in the holy place, and made the holy garments for Aharon; as the LORD commanded Moshe.

He made the efod of gold, blue, purple, scarlet, and fine twined linen. They beat the gold into thin plates, and cut it into wires, to work it in the blue, in the purple, in the scarlet, and in the fine linen, the work of the skillful workman.

They made shoulder straps for it, joined together. At the two ends it was joined together.

The skillfully woven band that was on it, with which to fasten it on, was of the same piece, like its work; of gold, of blue, purple, scarlet, and fine twined linen; as the LORD commanded Moshe.

They worked the shoham stones, enclosed in settings of gold, engraved with the engravings of a signet, according to the names of the children of Yisra'el.

He put them on the shoulder straps of the efod, to be stones of memorial for the children of Yisra'el, as the LORD commanded Moshe.

He made the breastplate, the work of a skillful workman, like the work of the efod; of gold, of blue, purple, scarlet, and fine twined linen.

It was square. They made the breastplate double.

Its length was a span, and its breadth a span, being double. They set in it four rows of stones.

A row of odem, pitdah, and bareket was the first row; and the second row, a nofek, a sappir, and an yahalom; and the third row, a lehshem, an shebu, and an akhlamah; and the fourth row, a tarshish, an shoham, and a yashefay. They were enclosed in gold settings.

Haftarah

1 Kings 8:6-8

> Parashat Pekudei
> Day 2

The Kohanim brought in the ark of the covenant of the LORD to its place, into the oracle of the house, to the most holy place, even under the wings of the Keruvim.

For the Keruvim spread forth their wings over the place of the ark, and the Keruvim covered the ark and the poles of it above.

The poles were so long that the ends of the poles were seen from the holy place before the oracle; but they were not seen outside: and there they are to this day.

Brit Chadasha

Hebrews 9:8-14

The Holy Spirit is indicating this, that the way into the Holy Place wasn't yet revealed while the first tabernacle was still standing; which is a symbol of the present age, where gifts and sacrifices are offered that are incapable, concerning the conscience, of making the worshipper perfect; being only (with meats and drinks and various washings) fleshly ordinances, imposed until a time of reformation.

But Messiah having come as a Kohen Gadol of the coming good things, through the greater and more perfect tabernacle, not made with hands, that is to say, not of this creation, nor yet through the blood of goats and calves, but through His own blood, entered in once for all into the Holy Place, having obtained eternal redemption.

For if the blood of goats and bulls, and the ashes of a heifer sprinkling those who have been defiled, sanctify to the cleanness of the flesh: how much more will the blood of Messiah, who through the eternal Spirit offered Himself without blemish to God, cleanse your conscience from dead works to serve the living God?

Parashat: Pekudei - "Accounts Of"

Daily Portion: Tuesday

Exodus 39:14-26

The stones were according to the names of the children of Yisra'el, twelve, according to their names; like the engravings of a signet, everyone according to his name, for the twelve tribes.

They made on the breastplate chains like cords, of braided work of pure gold. They made two settings of gold, and two gold rings, and put the two rings on the two ends of the breastplate.

They put the two braided chains of gold in the two rings at the ends of the breastplate.

The other two ends of the two braided chains they put on the two settings, and put them on the shoulder straps of the efod, in the front of it.

They made two rings of gold, and put them on the two ends of the breastplate, on the edge of it, which was toward the side of the efod inward.

They made two rings of gold, and put them on the two shoulder straps of the efod underneath, in the front of it, close by its coupling, above the skillfully woven band of the efod.

They bound the breastplate by its rings to the rings of the efod with a lace of blue, that it might be on the skillfully woven band of the efod, and that the breastplate might not come loose from the efod, as the LORD commanded Moshe.

He made the robe of the efod of woven work, all of blue. The opening of the robe in the midst of it was like the opening of a coat of mail, with a binding around its opening, that it should not be torn.

They made on the skirts of the robe pomegranates of blue, purple, scarlet, and twined linen.

They made bells of pure gold, and put the bells between the pomegranates around the skirts of the robe, between the pomegranates; a bell and a pomegranate, a bell and a pomegranate, around the skirts of the robe, to minister in, as the LORD commanded Moshe.

Haftarah

1 Kings 8:9

There was nothing in the ark save the two tables of stone which Moshe put there at Chorev, when the LORD made a covenant with the children of Yisra'el, when they came out of the land of Egypt.

Parashat Pekudei — Day 3

Brit Chadasha

Revelation 11:1-6

A reed like a rod was given to me.

Someone said, "Rise, and measure God's temple, and the altar, and those who worship in it.

Leave out the court which is outside of the temple, and don't measure it, for it has been given to the nations.

They will tread the holy city under foot for forty-two months.

I will give power to my two witnesses, and they will prophesy one thousand two hundred sixty days, clothed in sackcloth."

These are the two olive trees and the two menorot, standing before the Lord of the earth.

If anyone desires to harm them, fire proceeds out of their mouth and devours their enemies.

If anyone desires to harm them, he must be killed in this way.

These have the power to shut up the sky, that it may not rain during the days of their prophecy.

They have power over the waters, to turn them into blood, and to strike the earth with every plague, as often as they desire.

Parashat: Pekudei – "Accounts Of"

Daily Portion: Wednesday

Exodus 39:27-43

Parashat Pekudei — Day 4

They made the coats of fine linen of woven work for Aharon, and for his sons, and the turban of fine linen, and the linen headbands of fine linen, and the linen breeches of fine twined linen, and the sash of fine twined linen, and blue, and purple, and scarlet, the work of the embroiderer, as the LORD commanded Moshe.

They made the plate of the holy crown of pure gold, and wrote on it a writing, like the engravings of a signet: "HOLY TO THE LORD."

They tied to it a lace of blue, to fasten it on the turban above, as the LORD commanded Moshe.

Thus all the work of the tent of the tent of meeting was finished.

The children of Yisra'el did according to all that the LORD commanded Moshe; so they did.

They brought the tent to Moshe, the tent, with all its furniture, its clasps, its boards, it bars, its pillars, its sockets, the covering of rams' skins dyed red, the covering of sea cow hides, the veil of the screen, the ark of the testimony with its poles, the mercy seat, the table, all its vessels, the show bread, the pure menorah, its lamps, even the lamps to be set in order, all its vessels, the oil for the light, the golden altar, the anointing oil, the sweet incense, the screen for the door of the Tent, the bronze altar, its grating of brass, its poles, all of its vessels, the basin and its base, the hangings of the court, its pillars, its sockets, the screen for the gate of the court, its cords, its pins, all the instruments of the service of the tent, for the tent of meeting, the finely worked garments for ministering in the holy place, the holy garments for Aharon the Kohen, and the garments of his sons, to minister in the Kohen's office.

According to all that the LORD commanded Moshe, so the children of Yisra'el did all the work.

Moshe saw all the work, and behold, they had done it as the LORD had commanded, even so had they done it: and Moshe blessed them.

Haftarah
1 Kings 8:10-13

Parashat Pekudei — Day 4

It came to pass, when the Kohanim were come out of the holy place, that the cloud filled the house of the LORD, so that the Kohanim could not stand to minister by reason of the cloud; for the glory of the LORD filled the house of the LORD.

Then spoke Shlomo, the LORD has said that He would dwell in the thick darkness.

I have surely built you a house of habitation, a place for You to dwell in forever.

Brit Chadasha
Revelation 11:7-13

When they have finished their testimony, the beast that comes up out of the abyss will make war with them, and overcome them, and kill them.

Their dead bodies will be in the street of the great city, which spiritually is called Sedom and Egypt, where also their Lord was crucified.

From among the peoples, tribes, languages, and nations people will look at their dead bodies for three and a half days, and will not allow their dead bodies to be laid in a tomb.

Those who dwell on the earth rejoice over them, and they will be glad.

They will give gifts to one another, because these two prophets tormented those who dwell on the earth.

After the three and a half days, the breath of life from God entered into them, and they stood on their feet.

Great fear fell on those who saw them. I heard a loud voice from heaven saying to them, "Come up here!"

They went up into heaven in the cloud, and their enemies saw them. In that day there was a great earthquake, and a tenth of the city fell.

Seven thousand people were killed in the earthquake, and the rest were terrified, and gave glory to the God of heaven.

Parashat: Pekudei - "Accounts Of"

Daily Portion: Thursday

Exodus 40:1-16

The LORD spoke to Moshe, saying, "On the first day of the first month you shall raise up the tent of the Tent of Meeting.

You shall put the ark of the testimony in it, and you shall screen the ark with the veil.

You shall bring in the table, and set in order the things that are on it.

You shall bring in the menorah, and light the lamps of it.

You shall set the golden altar for incense before the ark of the testimony, and put the screen of the door to the tent.

You shall set the altar of burnt offering before the door of the tent of the tent of meeting.

You shall set the basin between the tent of meeting and the altar, and shall put water therein.

You shall set up the court around it, and hang up the screen of the gate of the court.

You shall take the anointing oil, and anoint the tent, and all that is in it, and shall make it holy, and all its furniture: and it will be holy.

You shall anoint the altar of burnt offering, with all its vessels, and sanctify the altar: and the altar will be most holy.

You shall anoint the basin and its base, and sanctify it.

You shall bring Aharon and his sons to the door of the tent of meeting, and shall wash them with water.

You shall put on Aharon the holy garments; and you shall anoint him, and sanctify him, that he may minister to me in the Kohen's office.

You shall bring his sons, and put coats on them. You shall anoint them, as you anointed their father, that they may minister to Me in the Kohen's office.

Their anointing shall be to them for an everlasting priesthood throughout their generations."

Moshe did so. According to all that the LORD commanded him, so he did.

Haftarah

1Kings 8:14-16

Parashat Pekudei — Day 5

The king turned his face about, and blessed all the assembly of Yisra'el: and all the assembly of Yisra'el stood.

He said, Blessed be the LORD, the God of Yisra'el, who spoke with His mouth to David your father, and has with His hand fulfilled it, saying, since the day that I brought forth My people Yisra'el out of Egypt, I chose no city out of all the tribes of Yisra'el to build a house, that My name might be there; but I chose David to be over My people Yisra'el.

Brit Chadasha

Revelation 15:5-6

After these things I looked, and the temple of the tabernacle of the testimony in heaven was opened.

The seven angels who had the seven plagues came out, clothed with pure, bright linen, and wearing golden sashes around their breasts.

Parashat: Pekudei - "Accounts Of"

Daily Portion: Friday

Exodus 40:17-38

Parashat Pekudei — Day 6

It happened in the first month in the second year, on the first day of the month, that the tent was raised up.

Moshe raised up the tent, and laid its sockets, and set up the boards of it, and put in the bars of it, and raised up its pillars.

He spread the covering over the tent, and put the roof of the tent above on it, as the LORD commanded Moshe. He took and put the testimony into the teivah, and set the poles on the ark, and put the mercy seat above on the ark.

He brought the ark into the tent, and set up the veil of the screen, and screened the ark of the testimony, as the LORD commanded Moshe. He put the table in the tent of meeting, on the side of the tent northward, outside of the veil. He set the bread in order on it before the LORD, as the LORD commanded Moshe. He put the menorah in the tent of meeting, opposite the table, on the side of the tent southward.

He lit the lamps before the LORD, as the LORD commanded Moshe. He put the golden altar in the tent of meeting before the veil; and he burnt incense of sweet spices on it, as the LORD commanded Moshe.

He put up the screen of the door to the tent. He set the altar of burnt offering at the door of the tent of the tent of meeting, and offered on it the burnt offering and the meal offering, as the LORD commanded Moshe.

He set the basin between the tent of meeting and the altar, and put water therein, with which to wash. Moshe, Aharon, and his sons washed their hands and their feet there.

When they went into the tent of meeting, and when they came near to the altar, they washed, as the LORD commanded Moshe. He raised up the court around the tent and the altar, and set up the screen of the gate of the court.

So Moshe finished the work. Then the cloud covered the tent of meeting, and the glory of the LORD filled the tent. Moshe wasn't able to enter into the tent of meeting, because the cloud stayed on it, and the LORD's glory filled the tent.

When the cloud was taken up from over the tent, the children of Yisra'el went onward, throughout all their journeys; but if the cloud wasn't taken up, then they didn't travel until the day that it was taken up.

For the cloud of the LORD was on the tent by day, and there was fire in the cloud by night, in the sight of all the house of Yisra'el, throughout all their journeys.

Haftarah

1Kings 8:17-21

Parashat Pekudei — Day 6

Now it was in the heart of David my father to build a house for the name of the LORD, the God of Yisra'el.

But the LORD said to David my father, Whereas it was in your heart to build a house for My name, you did well that it was in your heart: nevertheless you shall not build the house; but your son who shall come forth out of your body, he shall build the house for My name.

The LORD has established His word that He spoke; for I am risen up in the room of David my father, and sit on the throne of Yisra'el, as the LORD promised, and have built the house for the name of the LORD, the God of Yisra'el.

There have I set a place for the ark, in which is the covenant of the LORD, which He made with our fathers, when He brought them out of the land of Egypt.

Brit Chadasha

Revelation 15:7-8

One of the four living creatures gave to the seven angels seven golden bowls full of the wrath of God, who lives forever and ever.

The temple was filled with smoke from the glory of God, and from His power.

No one was able to enter into the temple, until the seven plagues of the seven angels would be finished.

Parashat: Pekudei - "Accounts Of"

Daily Portion: Shabbat Special Reading

Psalm 68:1-35

<<For the Chief Musician. A Psalm by David. A song.>> Let God arise! Let His enemies be scattered! Let them who hate Him also flee before Him.

As smoke is driven away, so drive them away. As wax melts before the fire, so let the wicked perish at the presence of God.

But let the righteous be glad. Let them rejoice before God. Yes, let them rejoice with gladness.

Sing to God! Sing praises to His name! Extol Him who rides on the clouds: to the LORD, His name! Rejoice before Him!

A Father of the fatherless, and a defender of the widows, is God in His holy habitation.

God sets the lonely in families. He brings out the prisoners with singing, but the rebellious dwell in a sun-scorched land.

God, when You went forth before Your people, when You marched through the wilderness... Selah.

The earth trembled. The sky also poured down rain at the presence of the God of Sinai-- at the presence of God, the God of Yisra'el.

You, God, sent a plentiful rain. You confirmed Your inheritance, when it was weary.

Your congregation lived therein. You, God, prepared Your goodness for the poor.

The Lord announced the word. The ones who proclaim it are a great company.

"Kings of armies flee! They flee!" She who waits at home divides the spoil, while you sleep among the campfires, the wings of a dove sheathed with silver, her feathers with shining gold. When the Almighty scattered kings in her, it snowed on Tzalmon.

The mountains of Bashan are majestic mountains. The mountains of Bashan are rugged.

Why do you look in envy, you rugged mountains, at the mountain where God chooses to reign? Yes, the LORD will dwell there forever.

The chariots of God are tens of thousands and thousands of thousands. The Lord is among them, from Sinai, into the sanctuary.

You have ascended on high. You have led away captives. You have received gifts among men, yes, among the rebellious also, that the LORD God might dwell there.

Blessed be the Lord, Who daily bears our burdens, even the God who is our salvation. Selah.

God is to us a God of deliverance. To the LORD, the Lord, belongs escape from death.

Parashat Pekudei

Day 7

But God will strike through the head of his enemies, the hairy scalp of such a one as still continues in his guiltiness.

The Lord said, "I will bring you again from Bashan, I will bring you again from the depths of the sea;

That you may crush them, dipping your foot in blood, that the tongues of your dogs may have their portion from your enemies."

They have seen Your processions, God, even the processions of my God, my King, into the sanctuary.

The singers went before, the minstrels followed after, in the midst of the ladies playing with timbrels,

"Bless God in the congregations, even the Lord in the assembly of Yisra'el!"

There is little Binyamin, their ruler, the princes of Yehudah, their council, the princes of Zevulun, and the princes of Naftali.

Your God has commanded your strength. Strengthen, God, that which You have done for us.

Because of Your temple at Yerushalayim, kings shall bring presents to You.

Rebuke the wild animal of the reeds, the multitude of the bulls, with the calves of the peoples. Being humbled, may it bring bars of silver. Scatter the nations that delight in war.

Princes shall come out of Egypt. Kush shall hurry to stretch out her hands to God.

Sing to God, you kingdoms of the earth! Sing praises to the Lord! Selah.

To Him who rides on the heaven of heavens, which are of old; behold, He utters His voice, a mighty voice.

Ascribe strength to God! His excellency is over Yisra'el, His strength is in the skies.

You are awesome, God, in Your sanctuaries. The God of Yisra'el gives strength and power to His people.

Praise be to God!

Published by

Tzedek Shuva Ministries

All Rights Reserved

"It is written, 'Man shall not live by bread alone, but by every word that proceeds out of the mouth of God.'"

Matthew 4:4

© 2010, Tzedek Shuva Ministries

www.tzedekshuva.org

Wisdom Cries Out

My son, if you will receive my words, and store up my mitzvot within you; So as to turn your ear to wisdom, and apply your heart to understanding; Yes, if you call out for discernment, and lift up your voice for understanding; If you seek her as silver, and search for her as for hidden treasures: then you will understand the fear of the LORD, and find the knowledge of God. For the LORD gives wisdom. Out of His mouth comes knowledge and understanding.

Proverbs 2:1-6

Tzedek Shuva Ministries
Addison, TX 75001

Made in the USA
Las Vegas, NV
19 July 2021